THE RETIREE

On to Geezerhood

by Jerry Hoem

PUBLISH AMERICA

PublishAmerica
Baltimore

ISBN: 1-4241-3547-8
PUBLISHED BY PUBLISHAMERICA, LLLP
www.publishamerica.com
Baltimore

Printed in the United States of America

This collection of articles is dedicated to my lovely wife Beth, who not only brought my writing to the attention of the local paper, but, uncomplaining, put up with my sitting at the computer at odd times when she wanted to use it. She must love me. I love her.

ACKNOWLEDGEMENTS

Thanks to the editor and publisher of *The Maple Lake Messenger,* Theresa Andrus, for indulging me in this silly hobby. It's a great way to be retired.

Prologue

"Whatever possessed you to send those columns to the local paper, anyway?" That's what I heard from a few people who don't understand just what a retiree does. My response was to ignore them, and just go on sending columns to the local paper.

Few of those naysayers could look back on five retirements as I can, so I figured I'm the pre-eminent retiree for the entire township. I haven't had any successful challenges. Who'd want to challenge that?

Getting retired was no trick in my case. Several firms seemed dedicated to making me retired. Becoming re-employed was the trick. There was a time when becoming re-employed was a driving force in my life, and I have records someplace of maybe three hundred resumes and applications to prove it.

But there's a time to sit back and be retired. When one decides it's finally time to do that, one can observe the little quirks and foibles and problems and failings and peculiarities that are everywhere. And if they aren't there, being retired means you can create them yourself! That's the beauty of retirement. Finally, you can take advantage of those quirks that got you in trouble during your working career, and delight in them.

My book is a compendium of retirement projects and work and relaxation and frustration and gratification and introspection and illness and wellness. Enjoy it. I enjoyed writing it.

Jerry Hoem

The Retiree—January, 2002—Sizes

My latest retirement is proving to be the most challenging of the five of them. Prospects of re-employment are dim, but to tell the truth I don't care. I am plenty busy running off to the dentist or doctor to complete payment books for their cars and boats. In my spare time between appointments, I try to define some of the more insignificant details of life that in the past only occurred to me in traffic jams or between planes.

One of the more important insignificant details of life that I have defined, at least for myself, has to do with size. Animal size, people size, and the size of other things, too, now that I think of it.

In South Carolina, our yard had several pines in the sixty to eighty foot range, and enough pecan and fig trees to provide energy for a squadron of squirrels. South Carolina squirrels seem to be about sixty percent smaller than Minnesota squirrels. South Carolina is about sixty percent smaller than Minnesota. Watching those little buggers fling themselves off my pine trees provided the germ of my theory. Bigger states have bigger animals. Smaller states have smaller animals. Where do you go for elk? Montana, or Alaska. Where are the oyster beds? Delaware, or Maryland. Where are the rats? New Jersey. Enough said.

As for people, that part of my theory extends to (and is to some extent derived from) the space allocated to people. The road to our condo in Connecticut was smaller by far than our South Carolina road was. And that road was smaller than County Road 37, near our place now. Our Connecticut condo was tiny, and my space at the office was smaller than that in either South Carolina or Minnesota. The lighting was worse, and the stapler was smaller, and the computer screen was smaller, too, than either South Carolina or Minnesota. The Scotch tape was narrower in Connecticut than in Minnesota, too. Really.

Minnesota has pontoon boats galore. Eight feet wide. New Hampshire has canoes. Two feet wide. And they brag about them. That's another thing. New England bragging. But that's another story. I've got a theory for that, too, but it can wait.

People are shorter in Connecticut, too, than they are in most other states. Look at Senator Lieberman, compared to, say, President Bush. That's because people are bigger in Texas than they are in Connecticut. In Rhode Island, they're really small. Some think it's because there are a lot of Portuguese there, but look at Portugal. Tiny, right? Proves my point.

There's an important international verification of my theory that I discovered in my travels for work. The first thing I observed upon landing in Germany (it was a LONG trip) was the fact that they have very narrow toilet paper. Sixty million people in a small country, and a fairly narrow one at that. No room for wide paper.

I'm content with my theory. I'm sure of my observations, and I have more of them, if anyone would ask. Nobody has asked yet, though, and my theory is about nine years old now, but if anyone would ask, I could come up with some more examples, such as those little French Citroen "duck" cars that are about three feet wide, but the point is proven anyhow. So what, you're probably asking. Who cares?

Well, no longer do you have to trust accents to tell where anyone came from. Just look at their size, or the width of their lapels, or whether they have big hair or not. No more "You're from Big D, I can guess, by the way you talk and the way you dress..." when you can just look at their size, or the size of their staplers. With a little practice, a glance will tell you if they're from Vermont or Georgia or Arizona.

Of course, it won't hurt if you hear them say "uff da" or "ayup" or "y'all" a few times.

The Retiree—January, 2002—Retirements

A few years ago, during my third retirement, I chose to write a column for "Midlands Maturity," a little-known paper produced monthly in Columbia, South Carolina. I called the column "A Minnesota Yankee in King Cotton's Court," a name the editor usually ignored but which I thought was pretty clever. The column became too much to deal with when I found employment in Connecticut, and besides, if I'd continued, the editor would have had to deal with a *real* Yankee. That would have been difficult, given the still-active status of the War of Northern Aggression, known hereabouts as the Civil War.

During my fourth retirement, I wrote a novel that is languishing in the top drawer of my credenza, awaiting a renewal of my enthusiasm for selling (which was lost before my second retirement). The novel borrows from life, mine, specifically my first three retirements, in developing a background for a murder, not mine.

Now in my fifth and presumably last retirement, my wife and I have returned to Minnesota as Lakers, parked firmly on Maple Lake, currently in our fifth year of bringing an old cabin into condition for human habitation.

Seems that whenever I retire, I get a bug to put my reminiscences on paper. It does keep me from indulging in plumbing repairs. My travels, mostly in pursuit of employment, have made me something of an observer of people, and I've become aware that most of the people I've worked with have been odd in one way or another. They'd possibly conclude the same about me. Having spent some idle retirement time in the Old South and in the Yankee stronghold of Connecticut, I've also found some fertile ground for comparing regional differences in the places that have possibly the most profound regional differences of any in the country.

One regional difference concerns waving. I find that, as a Laker, I'm back in waving territory. Minnesota waving. Minnesota one-finger waves are done with three fingers and the thumb of the hand on the steering wheel, and the waving finger is the point finger, not the middle. Greetings are extended when on foot if in a town of less than 25,000 people. If in a larger city, New England rules, modified by Scandinavian sincerity, apply (see below).

In the Old South, waving is required when driving, and it is done with the forearm and a flexed wrist, not too fast, genteel and friendly. A salute may be substituted for a wave, particularly when wearing a baseball cap. On foot, one is required to greet the oncoming person orally with a "good mawning" or other suitable greeting. This is done regardless of that oncoming person's color, contrary to the usual impression Northerners have about Southerners. And it must be done with a sincere smile.

In Connecticut, as in most of New England, waving from the car is often done at high speed with only one finger. One averts one's eyes when approaching another on foot, and certainly does not speak. In a building, you may greet fellow workers or relatives, if you do it coolly. Cool is important. There are differences within New England, of course. New Hampshire rural folks are different than inner-city Hartford folks; a little less harsh, a little friendlier. Even so, if your car sports a Connecticut plate, you'll be asked to leave your coat and bags by the door when you enter some establishments, just to make sure you don't steal the merchandise or attack a clerk. And you will follow New England waving rules, although possibly at a lower speed, and with a slightly different accent (e.g. Boston is "Bwaston" in Hartford, and

Hartford is "Haatfd" in Boston, and there are incremental differences between the two).

What this all boils down to is that I'm mighty glad to be settled into this place, and am working even yet at eliminating some of those other regional habits from my life. If you see someone wave inappropriately or talk to you on the street in a big city, accept my apologies ahead of time. It's probably me, and I'm still in training. Or rather in re-training.

The Retiree—February, 2002—Skyways

The other night about 8:30 we were driving from Buffalo to Maple Lake and we decided to go through town to see what was happening. We took back roads. Buffalo was pretty dull, once we left the highway where we'd been eating ice cream. Buffalo isn't a Wednesday-night town. There were some lights, but for the most part it was shut down. Maple Lake wasn't really swinging either. There was one truck parked by the laundromat. That's all. A recent article in *The Messenger* reflects the same observation of inactivity---and fear that it could get even worse.

I wondered, what's going on here? Rather, what isn't? Why are things so slow? Then the answer occurred to me. Minneapolis has a lot of activity, and a lot of skyways. St. Paul has almost as much activity, and a lot of skyways, too. Even Duluth has activity, and one of the longest skyways in creation, over by the curling club, if memory serves me correctly. Buffalo has no skyways. Maple Lake has no skyways.

It became obvious to me. Skyways are the secret. Skyways attract and create activity. The more skyways you have, the busier the town becomes. Maple Lake, then, could become the Minneapolis of the lake country with the addition of skyways. Maple Lake would take a lot of that cosmopolitan lustre that Buffalo has, and slosh it all over town. Maple Lake could become the Las Vegas of Wright County.

The obvious place to build the first skyway would be from the costume shop to the coffee shop. Just think of all the traffic that could be generated between those two places. People would line up just to walk over that bridge. They'd hang out there to watch parades, or just to see the pickups go by. They'd go from the bookstore to the laundromat by way of the skyway and have a cup of coffee on the way. In costume.

Another obvious place for a skyway would be from downtown to the ball park. Not even Minneapolis has a skyway to the dome, and you know how much trouble that dome has been. That would be a real coup. Downtown to the ball park. It should start at the firebarn and go to the ball park. That would be the best of all routes. Then if there's a ball game and a fire breaks out, the firemen could use the skyway to get to the engines.

Years ago I remember a price tag of about quarter of a million for a skyway. That's a little high for Maple Lake, so we could tie the skyways to the lumberyard. The ball park skyway could go right through the lumberyard. They'd make it a point of pride. "Look at the skyway (skyways?) we built!" Probably wouldn't cost anybody else a thing. And they've got forklifts and nails and stuff to put it up with, too!

Come on, everyone! Let's all get behind the skyways. No more waiting for rush-hour traffic to clear. No more problems with the weather. Just hop on the skyway along with all those other people, and have a cup of coffee or read a book or do your laundry or go to the bank. Maybe not the bank, since it seems to be moving. But, come to think of it, why not the bank? Get across Highway 55 without waiting for a light. Buy a used car, do your banking, maybe go to the airport? Yes! The airport! We don't even need a light rail system. Just a skyway! The mind boggles! After that, the beach! And then, Monticello, Annandale, the world!

The Retiree—February, 2002—Travel

One thing I like about retirement is not having to ask for time off. Now my wife asks me why we aren't going somewhere.

So a few weeks ago we went somewhere. Thanks to the internet, we got really really cheap tickets to Atlanta, and thanks to a travel club we got a really really cheap car rental (an '88 Yugo). Our goal was Barefoot Bay in Florida, so we had to upgrade the car, since there are no Yugo dealerships in the western hemisphere any more, and any remaining Yugos aren't allowed out of town.

Barefoot Bay isn't on the Atlantic, but it's close. It is a community of double-wides and single-wides, occupied by people who are, let's say, seniors. Some would be less discreet and call them old. Or ancient. Or comatose. Each resident has a big four-door retirement car. You can tell how long they have been retired by the ages of the cars. Seventy Cadillac, thirty-two years retired. Ninety-five Lincoln, seven years retired. Forty-nine Packard, well, maybe a collector, maybe not.

I was struck by the similarities to Maple Lake, if you don't consider the ages of the people. For example, people are friendly there. Perhaps it's because many of them think they are meeting you for the first time even though they aren't. Activities in both places revolve around the water, although there it is salt water and here it is (mostly) fresh. Boats abound, although here they are twenty-foot pontoons and there they are six-hundred-foot cruise ships. The sky here is dotted with Cessnas and there with rockets.

Bag boys there use walkers to deliver groceries to your car. People pull out of driveways into your path, knowing you are going fifteen miles an hour even though you aren't. When someone is starting a car in a shopping center, don't worry about driving behind the car because it will likely be ten minutes before he or she gets buckled up. Wal-Mart has a waiting list for greeters. Grocery aisles are long on geriatric products and short on baby formula.

We spent a lot of time on the beach. The beach there is a thousand miles long and a hundred yards wide. Our beach on Maple Lake is sixty-four feet long and two feet wide, but it's made of the same stuff. In Fort Pierce or Vero Beach one doesn't find many bikinis, and if one did, one would most likely avert one's eyes. Failing eyesight is a blessing for those in Barefoot Bay.

Do *not* fly out of Atlanta on a Monday, as we did. Delta has a web page that tells about delays at airports. The delay posted on the internet for security in Atlanta on Monday needs two digits for estimated hours of delay. People get in line full and get on the plane hungry. Some have learned how to sleep standing up. If you fly from there, carry nothing metal, including tooth fillings. Drill sergeants at ATL (we retirees refer to airports by their code names) police the lines and order people to stand up straight and wipe that smile off your face, trooper, and button those buttons, or something about grass and lawnmowers. People seem to take that sort of abuse without complaint, even though the added security hasn't made a bit of difference in what goes on in the air. There are still people cramming steamer trunks in the overhead and carrying on quilts and babies and dogs and snorkel parkas and, now, lunch. I don't like ATL any more. Never did.

In between the Yugo and the Security Gestapo, we spent some time in the Old South. Some day I will make a few notes about the Old South. I grew to like the Old South. Savannah, Charleston, Columbia. Pines and palmettos. Southern barbecue. Spanish moss. Gardenias. Azaleas. There. I'm a little more relaxed now. I think I'll take a walk on the beach. In my bunny boots.

The Retiree—February, 2002—Repairs

Retirement means being able to do all those things that were hired out when you worked for a living. Retirement means *having* to do all those things that you *can't afford* to hire out any more. One of those things that I couldn't hire someone else to do was to update a bathroom.

For maybe thirty years the outdoor toilet was completely satisfactory for our lake place. A year ago my lovely wife made me tear the thing down. She'd ripped the door off the previous year and burned it, and even though the view was enhanced, that act reduced its utility substantially. It had become mainly a tool shed for some time before that, so I shouldn't have had the emotional attachment to it that I did. But it's over now.

We have one perfectly good bathroom, but I made the mistake of having it built in our new bedroom, not easily accessible to visitors. The bathroom added in 1964 had an old steel shower stall and plywood walls and a certain rustic look that my wife came to detest, and I must admit it didn't do much for the ambience of the place. So I dug in and began the remodeling.

"We're only going to do this once, so let's do it right," I heard. In fact, I may have uttered those words myself once or twice, before I found out what doing it right really meant. It meant tearing out the walls and finally burying bodies of box elder bugs from the infestation of about fifteen years ago. It meant buying expensive tile and some floor jacks to keep the floor upstairs. It meant fixing that window that was broken in about 1997 when we moved back to town. It meant rebuilding the rotting floor that showered our son when someone flushed while he was in the basement. It meant choosing colors and picking out borders and scraping up old flooring and putting up plasterboard and installing new lighting and figuring out what to do with the ceiling and not fishing and not playing golf and not going on trips.

My latest part of the project has been to grout tile. Everything that doesn't carry water has been tiled, and now has to be grouted. I expect before this is done to be the most accomplished groutist in the world, or at least the most accomplished groutist on the north shore of Maple Lake. Maybe the most accomplished groutist on the bay. Grouting is my life, for now. Grout and I are one, especially under my fingernails. I wore out my point finger on grout. Public thanks are due my neighbor who lent me his tile saw, although I now know why he wanted it out of his house. I will be cleaning it up and returning it as soon as practical, hoping never to borrow it again.

Once the ceiling is done, maybe this year, I will restrain myself from going into that bathroom again. I am eyeing the woods north of our house to find a quiet and private spot, just in case I have a need when the other bathroom is in use. I plan to pick a location where I can't see the outside repairs that I've been neglecting. For quite awhile, now.

The Retiree—February, 2002—Projects

Murphy's Law, if I'm not mistaken, says "If something can go wrong, it will." Lots of folks have expanded that law to include things that are not completely relevant, and I'm one of those folks. Murphy has taken up residence in my bathroom. My lovely wife's expectations of completion of The Bathroom Project, or TBP as it is known, have been frustrated time and time again, and while I have been taking the blame, it's really Murphy's fault.

A decision was made by the Bathroom Project Manager (me, the BPM) to secure the old plywood ceiling to the rafters, a simple task. Finishing nails were used originally to secure the plywood, and years of leaky roofs and winter frost rendered them unreliable and unable to support a new ceiling, even if only paint. The BPM informed the Bathroom Project Auditor (my wife, the BPA) of the decision to proceed with a Securing Process involving my battery-powered drill and leftover screws from the deck. Appropriate oral approval was received from the BPA, and the Planning Process for the Ceiling Sub-Project (PPCSP) began.

Screws remaining from The Deck Project (TDP) were unavailable, having been used to attach a flag holder to the garage, an extension cord for the Christmas lights, and some of Murphy's projects. I had to go to the hardware store for more screws, and to remember when I got there the reason for the trip, no small feat for a retiree. Murphy delayed the project for a full day, frustrating the PPCSP, since nobody would make a trip just for screws, and I had to wait for more things to be needed, one of which was a plan for the ceiling (the complete PPCSP itself). That plan required a review of all the ceiling stuff available in St. Cloud. A trip like that usually includes lunch, but this time was completed with the purchase of jellybeans only, a saving of about fifteen dollars. But I digress. Murphy got both BPM and BPA to St. Cloud for PPCSP and screws.

I finally started the CSP (Ceiling Sub-Project, of course), where I encountered a number of corollaries to Murphy's Law. The first corollary was that a ladder will not fit where a ladder is needed. Second is a more common corollary universal to all ladder work, namely that a person will never bring enough nails or screws up a ladder to finish any job. My plan is if I need one screw, I bring two. Knowing Murphy, I bring three. One drops from my hand on the way up the ladder and invariably rolls down the heat duct, the second squirts away from the desired location and goes down the shower drain, and the third misses the rafter. Murphy has me make another trip down and up the ladder.

The battery on the drill fails when the screw is an eighth of an inch from being seated. I have to go down the ladder, get the spare battery from the basement, find out that Murphy has killed it, and I recharge the one on the drill. That provides time to open e-mail, which ties up the phone line and brings a virus or worm, but that's another digression.

Most of the nails in the ceiling are protruding due to Murphy's work in the attic since 1964, so it's back down the basement steps to get the hammer. I know Murphy by now, so I am exceedingly careful to place the hammer on the floor between uses to avoid dropping it on the tile. Murphy won't get me with that one. Unfortunately, being a senior, that means when I need it I have to go back down the ladder and find it among the other things scattered around the floor.

I decide to use my stud finder to seek out the rafters. Back to the basement. The stud finder doesn't work because Murphy has disabled its battery connection. I fix the stud finder, only to find that Murphy's stomping around the attic has made the plywood too far from the rafters to do any good anyway. I resort to the primitive means of drilling a hundred holes in order to locate the invisible rafters. Then I repeat the plan for carrying screws detailed above.

I haven't detailed the minor inconveniences Murphy uses to delay work, such as stepping on screws barefoot, trying to find dropped nails, knocking the box of screws off the toilet seat and having to move the ladder to get at them, finding two-thirds of them, knocking the radio knob off with the leg of the ladder, kicking over the dry grout box left over from the Grout Sub-Project (GSP), misplacing the coffee cup, leaving the drill in the basement, having to fix the loose hammer head, repairing the ladder, getting sawdust in the hair and on the glasses, answering the phone (computer call), and going to the other bathroom for traditional reasons, always when hands are full of plaster or glue.

Obviously, without Murphy, I would have been done with TBP months ago. Remember if you're ever a BPM working on a PPCSP, it isn't your fault, it's Murphy's. Someone tell the BPA. She won't believe me any more.

The Retiree—March, 2002—Duties

I'm not sure yet, but I think the duties of a retiree include participating in and reacting to feminine activities. Since my fifth and presumably final retirement, I've been asked to assist in picking out colors and matching curtains with wallpaper and "please tell me if this red one goes with my red one." I didn't even know that she *had* a red one. There is an enhanced emphasis on noticing things, such as haircuts. I found out that posting a sign on the door saying "your new haircut looks nice" while the wife is out getting a haircut is not sufficient. I tried that.

Another activity in which I have relinquished the masculine imperative is watching television. I know that if it were left to me, the home decorating channel—I don't even know its official name—would never be shown. When things are slow on broadcast television, which is practically all the time, someone on the home decorating channel will be talking about putting up shower curtains or refinishing antique tables or visiting gardens. I'd watch the World War II channel or whatever its official name is if I had my way. Since I gave up, I've read a few books, such as all the Sherlock Holmes stories and most of the condensed books that were left here by whoever used the place in the absence of me or my parents before me. The books are copyrighted in the fifties or sixties, crisp and easily broken but that's all right since I'm the only one who will ever open them. Or ever has.

There are still some masculine endeavors that must be preserved, and have been. I still get to buy outboard gas and oil. I still go hunting. I still get to scare away the feral cats around here, with rocks or air guns or loud shouting or explosives. I still dig the worms. I still clean the fish. I still get to watch the neighbors build stuff. I blow snow and I mow grass and I have a nice garage in which to hide.

Maybe things around here have always been as they are now. It's just that I was at work and didn't realize what went on at home. That's got to be it. Nothing changed, except me. Now I don't have to put up with rush hours or bag lunches or two-dollar cappuccino or trips to who-knows-where or unfinished software or obstreporous bosses or impatient clients or dummies who can't find their behinds with both hands or people who are really smart and make me feel like I can't find my behind with both hands. Retirement has been a good trade-off. It doesn't pay well, but being retired is possibly the best job I've ever had.

Even though sometimes I don't know if she has a red one.

The Retiree—March, 2002—TYH

Water. That's what living at the lake is all about. But I thought that meant swimming and boating and fishing. When you are remodeling an old cabin to create a new house, that's not what it's all about. It's about water seeking its own level, about natural phenomena, about trying to get rid of mold, about leaks. Our particular water problems start at the roof and go to the basement.

Adding a room or two to what used to be not much more than a tepee or yurt or hovel causes a tepee/yurt/hovel (TYH? That's a good name for it) to go into something like shock. That's not a good condition for a TYH. Once when I was collecting for a charity an ancient lady with a cantankerous pen muttered to me about the "perversity of inanimate objects." That's what our house is doing to us. Being perverse.

When we arrived at TYH to begin our remodeling, it was early May and our heat source was a condemned fireplace. We awakened the house to our invasion by plugging in anything that would create heat and burning anything combustible regardless of the danger until the weather warmed up. One could almost hear TYH say "I'll get them for this."

Hooking roofs onto roofs provided us a continuing opportunity for leaks in TYH. One contractor objected to continuing with a new roof until we did something about the rotten old roof, for about two grand.

We consented. TYH responded well to the infusion of cash, with its only response being relocation of some gigantic icicles that had been, of course, no problem when we didn't heat the place.

A second contractor hooked another new roof onto an old one, but evidently didn't foresee that there could be an ice dam that would reach beyond the new flashing. We're still recovering from that. I really think that brown stains on the ceiling provide a visual emphasis that gives interest to an otherwise bland white expanse of plaster, but the wife disagrees.

A big rain gave us a chance to create Three Rivers Park, a canal system not unlike those in Florida or Holland or Venice, to channel rains around the house instead of through the basement. The park was created late at night during a cold three-inch rain, using shovels and rubber boots and ponchos and a lot of yelling to divert water from the well entrance a couple feet down the foundation of TYH. Water filled the crawl space and threatened to develop into a waterfall into the partial basement, which already had a creek running to the overhead door on the lake side. I had to batter a hole into the door so the creek could exit. One could hear the water running in the basement if one were quiet, but most of the time I was yelling. Since that flood subsided, the dikes have held. During the flood, though, we feared that TYH would wash into the lake, making it even wetter, but not much.

Some of our water problems originated indoors. Installing a washing machine provided an interesting fountain effect in the laundry room. A couple weeks of work with teflon tape and rubber washers eventually dried that up. New drains in the bathroom and kitchen were leaky challenges that we took in stride, even though sore elbows and backs developed. A sweaty toilet over the past thirty-five years rotted out a floor, creating dirty rainstorms in the basement, adding to the basement creek and raising the prospect of problems with the EPA and DNR. That problem was corrected so our son would once again bring his family to visit.

People say you live at a lake? How lovely! We say, yes, it's nice to be near water. We bite our lips and rub our weary muscles and suppress our tears. We mumble about the perversity of inanimate objects. Then we go out on the deck, listen to the chickadees and cardinals, watch the sun set, breathe the clean air, and, by golly, they're right. It really is lovely, after all.

The Retiree—April, 2002—Trips

My lovely wife and I made another trip. It seems that, instead of commuting, we now make trips that add up to the same number of miles that commuting did. This trip was to relatives on the Arkansas—Missouri border. That area of the Ozarks is famous for Branson and War Eagle and Eureka Springs and Silver Dollar City and rednecks and hillbillies. Don't tell my brother-in-law about the last two.

I enjoyed just sitting and listening to the locals talk. They had an interesting approach toward conversation, not unlike that in local barbershops and laundromats, but with a twist. For example, at the local hospital, in the dialysis waiting room—that's the place where retirees go when they visit other retirees—the technician asked one of the patients how he was today and the response was "Hain't wuth a damn. How y'all doin'?" And as another retiree left the premises, he was asked, "Whatcha gonna dew this afternoon?" The response was "Nothin'." That's all. Later in a restaurant I overheard a conversation by a slight, well-dressed lady that concluded, "Some a them coons is real big. An' mean. More'n once I seen 'em kill a dawg."

Houses down Arkansas way are not the backwoods shacks we expected. Most of the houses actually had their wheels taken off, as did almost all of the businesses, and some of them had been skirted as well. There were electric lines in evidence and most bathrooms were not in separate structures. A local radio station reported that while the governor's mansion was being refurbished, a *triple*-wide was installed on the grounds. Now, that's class. A *triple*-wide. But then he's the governor. He probably has a black extended-cab chauffeured pick-up.

Arkansas has progressed over the years, and people were driving vehicles that were post-war. Some of them were not even pick-ups. From time to time we were passed on the highway by the locals, usually in red pick-ups with dual rear wheels and chrome exhaust extensions. There was a junked Jaguar in the woods near the brother-in-law's house, proving that progress has been made for a number of years now.

My favorite restaurant is down in Berryville (pronounced Bar'vl). The landlord wouldn't fix the roof, so the tenants put up a sheet of corrugated metal inside, over the counter, that was slanted to drain into an eavestrough and downspout that led to the sink. It was really quite an engineering feat. Unfortunately it didn't rain while we were there.

Branson was interesting. Most of the vacationers we saw were World War II veterans, as were a good share of the entertainers. It seems that the bloom is off the rose there. One would guess the half-life of the audiences to be about ten years, and most of the ones still with us will be institutionalized in some manner by that time.

As broadening as travel is, we are glad to be back where lakes don't have an earthen dam on one end, and where people don't speak in a drawl, and where biscuits and gravy aren't first on the menu. We feel like we're nearing home when the landscape turns a little flatter and the radio stations don't fade out because of the hills and the waitresses don't have big hair. It will only be a short time until the Ozarks are hot and we aren't. But it was nice to see water again.

The Retiree—April 30, 2002—Absentees

Wife and I were sitting around in our retired state the other day, reminiscing about the wacky things that our house has witnessed through the years. Not so much about what happened lately, but things that happened earlier, in its pre-house days. Especially while we lived in South Carolina. Absentee ownership creates interesting tales.

We weren't always up to supervising a place from 1300 miles away. For instance, one day our daughter called us to ask permission to bring "a few people out after finals." Who, we said. People from the Seminary. Married couples, ministers, theology students, people like that. Responsible people. All right, we said, that's okay. By the way, how many, we asked. Thanks for permission, she said. How many, we repeated. Thirty, maybe thirty-five, she said. The place sleeps six. They'll bring sleeping bags, she said, and tents, and campers. They did, and they were responsible, and the neighbors said they enjoyed the singing around the campfire. We hope so. It must have sounded like the Mormon Tabernacle Choir. Several years later, people we never met still greet us with "We sure had a good time at your place back in '94." Or, '92, or '95, as there were other gatherings of lesser numbers.

We kept a log book over the years for visitors. It gave us a record of the various people who helped keep the place intact when we lived out of town. Here are examples:

=> "We're glad that's over, and nobody got hurt, and the rest of the

31

time went well." A year or so later, we found out that one of the visitors had fallen overboard and had gone down twice before they figured out that he couldn't swim.

=> "A pair of wood ducks fell down the fireplace chimney." We got a phone call on that one. Our son-in-law and a friend spent several hours cleaning every window in the place, picking feathers out of the curtains, scooping up duck contents from the floor, and disposing of a couple very dead ducks. Many years earlier Dad escorted a duck out of the house alive, a much better way to do it. We've upgraded the fireplace.

=> "We helped clean up that downed oak for you." That meant we wouldn't have the firewood we'd expected.

=> "We contributed logs to the wood pile." They were usually cottonwood, or maybe ironwood. Some of it burned. The rest rotted.

=> "Thanks for the good time. We scraped the old paint off your front door and grubbed out that stump." It was a tremendous, difficult effort. To this day we haven't admitted to them that we replaced the door shortly thereafter, and the tree that grew next to the stump blew over. Onto our pontoon boat.

Not everything was recorded in the book:

=>A Swedish student water skiing next door wrapped the rope around his arm just as someone said "Hit it." He was all right in a day or two.

=>Our son, at age three, took a header off the dock and scared the bejabbers out of Dad and a friend until they yanked him out by the hair. He said he couldn't breathe under there, a valuable lesson for everyone.

=>An unidentified animal skull was found in the well pit, probably a cat.

=>There's a muskrat buried by the lake, a drowned dog buried by the cornfield in back.

=>A lineman had to shoot a raccoon out of one of our trees, and a baby raccoon fell to his death on our driveway.

=>A backhoe operator managed to snag a rolling boulder he'd

unearthed just before it got away from him and entered our kitchen.

Winters have a calming effect on us. We're ready for summer now. But the log book has been put away. Some things are best forgotten.

The Retiree—June, 2002—Lists

Most, maybe all, Lakers have a prioritized list of things that have to be done around the house. It's part of living by a lake. The list may be in the form of a job jar, or it may be a mental list of those things that, if not completed by a certain date, will result in the complete eradication of their investment or collapse of the house or radical change in the world as we know it. Living in a former cottage that dates back to the fifties, my list is extensive. Some of the items on my list were inherited from my father.

Eliminating list items is difficult. All the things on the list have to be done, but maybe not today or tomorrow. Wife knows about some of the items, and those are sacrosanct. Forty years in the world of business showed me that only the top two or three items on any priority list really get done. A lot of the others become irrelevant as time goes by, or are superseded by completion of other items, or are made obsolete by technology, or are just plain loony ideas from upper management that won't be done in any case. Home lists are different, as they arise most often from some problem that won't go away.

Here are a few examples from the bottom of my list:

#304—Replace the handle on the push mower. It's held together with a muffler clamp and two self-tapping screws.

#305—Get the old *old* riding mower (Dad's mower) running. It's probably a blown head gasket or carburetion problem.

#306—Get the three-horse outboard running. Uncle Berney returned it after borrowing it for his lake place around 1956. He's ninety-three now and doesn't think he'll need it.

#307—Make bird houses out of the license plates and boards from the outdoor toilet. Some of the boards already have holes in them.

#308—Replace the crawl space light that someone kicked out in 1959. Dad's list.

#309—Grub out the basswood stump from the storm of 1997. This one is taking care of itself, the main way anything ever comes off the list when it's this far down. It's related to #314.

#310—Get the gas-powered line trimmer running. The electric one works fine, and doesn't need any maintenance. This could change places with #314.

#311—Replace the mailbox. It's still standing, so it's no big deal.

#312—Tuckpoint the fireplace chimney brick. I'm the only one who knows that this is on the list.

#313—Fix the leaky garden hose. All the rubber washers around here are rock-hard, older than my kids, and driving three miles for a washer is silly. After all, the grass gets watered anyway.

#314—Replace the handle on the spade. The adze handle is shot, too. These can both be moved up the list if the duct tape wears off the spade, although I have plenty of duct tape.

Priorities #1 through #303 were thoughtfully ranked. As you get down a list of hundreds of items, ranking becomes a little less important.

Some day I will think about the hose when I'm at the hardware store, and that will make me think about the spade handle and the stump, and bang, three items will drop off the list, assuming a little more stump rot.

How important is something three hundred items down the list, though? It took forty years to build the list, and it will probably take another forty to get it done. Maybe the kids will do it. Prioritization is more of a priority for them, and besides, they have newer rubber washers.

The Retiree—June, 2002—Trips

We took another trip. It's an obligation for retired people. Four thousand miles, including some backtracking and excluding trips in other people's cars. The trip was to meet a new grandson, and he's brilliant and adorable, just to get that out of the way. Already, at the age of one day, the new grandson re-routed our trip. We were scheduled to see friends in Oregon, but little Ian came a week ahead of schedule so we headed for Idaho. Oregon waited a couple weeks. Babysitting and household chores became our routine.

One chore was to bring the family to the dentist. The cast of characters at the dentist's office rivaled the bar scene in Star Wars. One lady with a tattoo was trying to go home, but she'd just moved to Boise and couldn't remember where she lived. Tattoo's roommate was surfing the net and couldn't be reached by phone. Tattoo left the office on three different occasions to try to solve her dilemma. A receptionist went after her to give her a ride, but couldn't find her. Tattoo reappeared again, and again. After three tries to find Tattoo, her rescuer gave up and went home. Another patient, wheelchair-bound, told the desk clerk that he had trouble with numbers since he hit that wall at eighty miles an hour, and he couldn't quite remember what month it was, but his mom would help. A man with a wheeled carry-on bag full of medications stopped by to see if he could get some pain medication that wouldn't interfere with the other fifteen or twenty bottles he had. A Basque lady called through the outside door for someone named Carrie. Took the day off, they called back. I need to see her, said the Basque. Can't, she isn't here. Need her home number, she said. Won't give it out. She then came in and searched all the offices for Carrie, emerging with a cup of water and going outside again, probably to return to her sheep fold. When we left the office, Tattoo was sitting on the ground by the bus stop, and she gave us a friendly wave. I'd like to return to that office again some day.

A truck on U.S. Highway 12 whacked us with a rock giving us a softball-sized smash that let us experience Boise windshield repair. Idaho still allows premiums to be given with repairs. We now have twenty-four meals at a Boise restaurant to be used up monthly by the end of the year, as well as a coupon for a diamond necklace. Collecting on the meals will cost us about sixteen thousand dollars if we get the NWA special fourteen-day advance airfare. The necklace will cost sixteen bucks for handling and insurance.

Oregon gave us spring and summer and winter one day when we drove eight thousand feet up Mount Hood. Snowboarders were complaining about the heat and sticky snow a couple thousand feet farther up the mountain. We were more interested in getting warm as we didn't have chains with us and the signs warning about chaining up were out. Evidently Oregon gets testy if you don't have chains with you. In June. They like rules in Oregon.

Idaho has a lot going for it. So do Oregon and Montana. Black bean soup, Basque bread, volcanic rock, blizzards, desert heat, some Junebug-sized things called Mormon crickets, full rivers, snow-capped mountains, snowplows (late May), frozen ponds, open swimming pools, bears, ten-thousand-foot passes. We also had to endure both Dakotas and their endless vistas of virtually nothing at all. On the way out, Kansas was returning all the dirt across the Dakotas that had blown down there in the winter from Canada, and on the way back, Canada was blowing in new spring storms for Kansas. Wind is a way of life on the prairie.

A full night's sleep allows the eyes to return to normal focus, and bodies, if forced, eventually regain something like a standing posture. I'm sure we'll go someplace again. I hope it's a little closer. Like maybe French Lake.

The Retiree—July, 2002—Reunion

From time to time we get together with some of my bride's siblings, to check on who's mad at whom, who bought something new, whose kid got laid off or jailed or pregnant. These episodes are at once interesting and confusing, especially to sister-in-law Arlene and me. The two of us long ago decided not to worry about names and places that come up in these sessions. We smile and nod and agree with the consensus about whoever is being discussed. This detachment has served us well, although from time to time we have been embarrassed by faulty recollections.

Faulty recollections are a help when making notes about these get-togethers. I plainly don't care about accuracy. Given that understanding, here's a faulted record of the last meeting, held in a restaurant in Hutch, a neutral site. I didn't attach names to the quotes because you don't know them, and in fact I don't know very many of them either, not that it matters.

"I heard that Frank Ausgehen died last winter."

"Wasn't dead when I saw him this morning."

"Did you bring your trailer and some cows this time?"

"All the cows stayed home. I got a length of chain and some apples, though. And some relish."

"I brought relish too. You didn't make it to the reunion, did you?"

"Did too make the reunion. Left early, before Gus came."

"Gus didn't come, did he?"

"Yah he did. Spent the day playing backgammon with Rose's kid in the gazebo where he wouldn't have to talk to Bill and Sara. You heard about the blowup at Young Ben's funeral."

"Young Ben died at ninety-one. Old Ben died fifty years ago and they still called him Young Ben. Carried the name to his grave."

"Good thing someone carried it. The dang wind was so strong it took the casket away from the pall bearers and blew it half way to county road three. Traffic was light on the highway, though."

"I'm Margaretha Belle Hamilton, and I'll be your server. Can I get you anything?"

"Ya. Get me a dozen eggs and a jar of relish out of the silver Sable in the parking lot."

"Get me an order of them chips and cheese with extra salsa, Margaretha Bill."

"That's Belle, and I don't do eggs and relish."

"Been to the sale in the mall over there? Sponges for four bits, eight-track tapes, double-knit slacks, too."

"Which kids are in Texas now, besides your girl?"

"Probably Todd and Steve and Ollie, and maybe Verna."

"Verna and Todd are in Charleston now, and Blake's putting up with her and her kid."

"Kid? When'd that happen? Blake's in Charleston?"

"Couple years ago; divorced now, and so's Ralph."

"Ralph? They been married forty years."

"Not that Ralph. Esther's Ralph. Red-haired Ralph with the bad teeth. Young Ralph. Old Ralph's in Kansas."

"Don't start that young—old stuff again. I thought Old or Big or Non-Red Ralph was in Oregon."

"Laid off. Moved to Wichita. Or Topeka. Near Jan and Dick."

"Jan and Dick are in Tulsa. Pass the chips."

"Shawnee. Saw them in Eagle Rock in April. Ken and Barb think they're spoiled but Ken's been jealous ever since graduation."

"Hers? Or his?"

"Hers. She kept the car, you know. Needed a piston so she fixed it. Still junk."

"I got everything on one check. Pay me when you're ready. I'm going off my shift."

"Come back Tuesday, Margie Bill, after we get it split up, and put your shift back on."

There was a lot of other talk about chain and cheese and relish and eggs, but you're probably as tired of it as Arlene and I were. We would have left, but our spouses won't let us go off together any more. There'll be another get-together as soon as something significant happens. Maybe I'll bring a tape recorder.

The Retiree—July, 2002—Parable

In the process of bringing my "new" old computer up to date (it failed me again and I had to get a major overhaul) I found some important papers in a file of documents from the past. One of my cohorts and I at the software factory where we worked occasionally created things of very little utility for the company. Creations of this type serve to keep often-perplexed employees relatively sane. Those who don't comport themselves in such a manner are often carted off to mental care facilities. Our elegant comprehensive hard-copy booklet of writings, composed of discarded report covers and green-stripe paper, has disappeared. Fragments still remain, a little like the Dead Sea Scrolls. I found one such fragment. Here it is, from the book "Fables for the Technically Impaired" (unpublished, but very high in concept and nominally high in structure). It's a modern corporate fable dealing with Corporate Thought, called…

THE FABLE OF THE MILK BUCKET.

Once upon a time, in the Kingdom of Acronia, there dwelt in a grand cubicle a High Tech Guru whose domain of expertise extended into the deepest realms of Corporate Organization. This Guru's fame had extended well beyond Acronia; his perspicacity was admired by all. The Guru had a young novitiate whose goal was to learn all he could about the dark and complex world of corporate organization. The student frequently approached his Guru with perplexing questions found so often in large organizations, and was always rewarded (most of the time condescendingly) with great gems of wisdom, like unto those so often pronounced in large organizations. For, indeed, a great share of the Guru's wisdom had come from those large organizations.

On one occasion, the student brought a particularly difficult question to the Guru. He inquired, "Master, please explain the basic concepts of the importance of the individual to the organization. How does an organization utilize the enormous variety of experience held by its members to the advantage of the whole? How does each individual's experience contribute to and become a part of that whole?"

The Guru was annoyed by the novitiate's question, but also challenged by the chance to reveal his acumen. He reflected for a moment; then said, "Picture the corporation as a bucket of milk. And visualize your arm as one individual; a member of that organization. Thrust your arm into that bucket of milk and in doing so simulate the individual's joining the organization. As the arm enters the bucket of milk, its identity disappears into that of the milk. It cannot be seen as an arm. It becomes one with the milk. The bucket becomes the whole. The arm is one with the milk, as the individual is one with the corporation."

"I see," said the student. "And what if the corporation and the individual should part company? What of that? What then becomes of the individual's knowledge?"

The Guru pronounced, in his most corporate and professorial tone, "Withdrawing the arm leaves a hole but for an instant. The hole is quickly filled, and the corporation resumes its original form, accumulating the knowledge of many into its entirety once again."

"I see. Ah, true," said the student. "But, Master, is not the level of the milk at least a little lower, once the arm is removed? What of that? What of that reduction in the level of milk?"

The Guru once again appeared annoyed by his novitiate. He had to rid himself of the annoyance and still preserve his ranking as High-Tech Guru. He closed his eyes for a moment, crossed his arms, and, laying a finger upon

43

his cheek, contemplated his student's question. Then, slowly he opened his eyes. The novitiate was still there. Once again, he closed his eyes to ponder. Once again when he opened them the novitiate remained. He knew he must answer.

Taking a deep breath, he finally announced quietly, "Shoot, I dunno. I never thought of that before."

The two of us cohorts are no longer at that software factory, probably not because of the above. We both moved on to other endeavors. Some of them were successful, some not. We can look back on our checkered pasts, though, with the knowledge that with our observations we made an enduring contribution to society. Or maybe not. But then, five hundred years from now, who'll know the difference?

The Retiree—July, 2002—Work

A friend called the other day with a request for me to work. I remember work, and it usually wasn't all that bad. This friend owns a courier business, and has learned to eat, drive, talk on the phone, and write all at once, while deciding how to route himself and a half-dozen drivers all over the Twin Cities. Once before, when he was on vacation, I handled the business for a week. I emerged with a feeling that he had mastered something that I couldn't master, and further didn't care to master. But once again I said yes.

Each time I say yes to this friend, I end up with enough adventure to last me a few months. No need to mention the wacky drivers out there. Everyone knows about them. The events that are worth mentioning this time have to do with the changing city.

I got to see the whole city. Blaine to Eagan, South St. Paul to Plymouth and beyond. The most interesting places are still inner city sites, such as Frogtown and Lowertown and Nordeast, and Bryn Mawr which with road construction is nearly impossible to find.

One of my stops was at a Frogtown grocery, where I picked up ten boxes of plastic material in fragile Oriental cardboard boxes. The store was operated by some accented people who could have been Vietnamese, or maybe Thai, or, who knows, Korean. The clientele was generally African, really African, not African American, speaking native tongues that were completely unintelligible to me. Products in the store were labeled with names I had never seen before and couldn't read. Smells in the store resembled food of some sort, nothing that I could identify. Tall people in native dress, people who looked like National Geographic Watusis, were buying bags of rice and boxes of who-knows-what. The thin little lady at the register was talking on the phone and viewed customer service as an unwelcome intrusion into her private life. Old shiny muscle cars, lowered, with chrome seventeen-inch wheels and similarly sized sound system speakers, populated by people wearing flop hats and dashikis, drove around the neighborhood. I was fascinated. Why the Oriental grocery was shipping plastic that smelled of fish remained unexplained even after I delivered the boxes to Blaine. It ain't the Frogtown of old. I put Frogtown on my list of places to take out-of-town visitors.

Franklin Avenue is now a Spanish-speaking enclave rather than the Native American area that I expected. I've been to San Juan so I was fairly comfortable. Signs in the business windows say "English spoken here."

Post offices were on my route. The downtown St. Paul post office allows anyone to walk in and wander around with impunity. A few miles away, the Bulk Facility of the post office makes you phone from a gate, drive to another door, ring for admission, exhibit an identity card, and be asked your business. Semi drivers are faced with more intimidation by some officials behind bulletproof glass. Very secure, until you realize that I used someone else's identity card to get in. I don't feel any safer for that.

There's a business in Fridley that banks in South St. Paul. South and West St. Paul don't seem to have changed much from the days when I cared about things like that. There's still no reason why they are called South and West, as they don't seem to be either. Fridley has a bunch of new industry hidden behind the old Fridley. I didn't want to ask the Fridley business why it's necessary to bank in South St. Paul for fear that my friend would lose an account. There's a copy shop in Blaine that makes copies for the St. Paul post office and I don't want to ask them why either, for the same reason. Once we took a CD full of ad data to a print facility, although some technology would do it instantly for practically nothing, and the mailman could make deliveries tomorrow for a whole lot less than a courier.

But, my job was to drive. So I drove. And drove. The next day I didn't drive much at all. Maybe I will again, some day. Maybe if we have visitors who want to see Frogtown. Not soon, though. I need a rest.

The Retiree—July, 2002—Beeps

Being a retiree on the lake means that one assumes daytime duties that weren't anticipated before retirement. For example, one must make sure none of the neighborhood boats floats away when their absent owners fail to use retiree-approved knots to tie them up. Recent rains and winds have increased the need for diligence in this regard. I tied up three escaping boats in July and am planning a knot-tying class for the fall.

Another duty is to trace strange noises to their sources and do one's best to rectify their causes. This problem appeared the other day, when a "beep-beep-beep (pause) beep-beep-beep..." came from someplace. Clever detective work on my part traced its source to the next-door neighbor's kitchen. Evidently either the smoke alarm was malfunctioning, or their kitchen was on fire. I called and left a message asking him to call 911 if the second eventuality turned out to be the true one. It wasn't. The beep-beep-beep quit by itself after a long but undetermined period of time.

Surprisingly, the beep-beep-beep resumed the next day. Perhaps it was programmed to start when certain conditions were met, such as a rise in humidity or a phase of the moon or the appearance of Martha Stewart on TV. Leaving messages on the phone for people forty miles away could be fruitless as they may be working or vacationing in Asia Minor or at the hospital or someplace else. Therefore I have developed a list of solutions for retirees who are faced with a beep-beep-beep or similar situation.

=> The Shotgun Approach: Poke out the window nearest The Offending Appliance (for purposes of this document call it TOA) and blast it into oblivion with a twelve-gauge. The disadvantage is noise and the possible involvement of law enforcement.

=> The Insulation Approach: Drill a small hole in the back door, insert the tube from a can of expanding foam insulation through the hole, and squirt. Repeat the operation until the room fills with insulation to the level of TOA. Could be messy. Expensive, too.

=> The Sprinkler Approach: Stick a hose nozzle through a hole drilled in the back door and turn on the water until it soaks the TOA into submission. Use the neighbor's water. A level of animus on the part of the neighbor could be anticipated.

=> The Earplug Approach: Cork up your ears and forget about TOA.

=> The Earth Mound Approach: A dump truck made two visits to a neighbor's driveway the other day when no one was around. I didn't disturb the process, but the loads could have been directed to the kitchen wall where TOA was most evident. Here again, animosity could be induced.

=> The Power Approach: Back your truck into their power line. If TOA happened to be battery-operated, the effectiveness of this approach could be diminished, unless the pole happened to fall on the kitchen. And, another problem, you may not have a truck. Also, the power company objects to this and similar actions as a matter of company policy.

Faced with the long-term nature of neighbors, I admit to the problems that could be generated by the approaches above. We like our neighbors and we would probably say that even if they didn't read *The Messenger* regularly. All but The Earplug Approach would seem to violate some sort of scruples. Maybe I'll have to follow the pattern I've learned to use in the past. That is, I'll just ignore it, and maybe go fishing.

I have, however, taped a transmitter-actuated battery-powered doorbell under the floor in the neighbor's crawl space. Ain't technology wonderful?

The Retiree—August, 2002—Trip

Here we go again. Another trip to Idaho. This one should be the last trip to Idaho for awhile, as we grandparents try to cope with the independent children we intended to raise.

Evidently we did a splendid job. The kid in Idaho has once again exhibited independence of a singular nature. Actually, it was her husband who did the exemplary job of exhibiting independence. He's a Lutheran pastor, and he accepted a call to take a congregation on St. Lucia in the Caribbean. We said, rather loudly, "Where?" and sure enough he said St. Lucia. Windward islands, south of practically everything, as close to Caracas as it is to Puerto Rico. We can drive to Idaho, we said, but not to the West Indies. Good, he said, when you drive to Idaho, there's some stuff we need to send back with you to store for us for a few years.

Throughout her college years we tried to get our only daughter to hang around country clubs and attract a rich husband. So she hung around a seminary. Another sign of independence, but it sure didn't pay off in free travel for us or in great wealth for her. We like the son-in-law, and wouldn't do anything to change things now, but there's an awful lot of money at Lafayette or Wayzata or even Golden Valley that is going unclaimed.

So anyway we fixed up the old Bronco and cleaned out the storage unit and prepared to take on a dog for a few years even though the dog has incredible energy and we don't, and the storage unit has only about four by seven feet of free space. That's all the Bronco can hold anyway. Although the service manager wouldn't commit himself directly, he seemed to think the old rust-bucket could take another four thousand miles of abuse.

Our first duty when we get to Idaho will be to babysit three grandchildren for a week while our kids go househunting in the Caribbean. They probably have someone on St. Lucia who will prepare new thatch for the roof and cut bamboo for the walls and get a spear for fishing or whatever they do there. Meanwhile we will be chasing grandchildren aged five and three and zero all over the Idaho foothills. Pray for us.

Over the past few years we've made friends in Wisconsin and Florida and Idaho through associations with our vagrant daughter's family. It'll be hard for us to say goodbye to them as well as to our family. We still hear consistently from a few people they introduced us to. Who knows, maybe there'll be some people on St. Lucia that we'll get to call friends.

But we'll have to get there first. There aren't any direct connections from MSP. The last leg of the trip could be via mail boat or tramp steamer. I will bring extra outboard oil when we finally go there. Some days I think we're getting too old for this.

But there are those winter days when the wind is off the lake and the snow is piling up around the garage…

The Retiree—August 2, 2002—Refinishing

I'm sure that my sister is chortling to herself about her cleverness in gettiing me to take another piece of furniture off her hands. Once she gave me an old ice box, and refinishing it caused me to miss many a social event. The final product has bad hardware and no legs, but people say it's nice. It was but a prelude.

Back in 1948 when Grandfather died, he left his oak secretary behind. The secretary provided a place for him to write letters and to put his bills until he paid them, which was always at the absolute last minute. The piece has a curved glass front that must have been protected by its own guardian angel considering all the years it's been around. The guardian angel went with the secretary to Dad and Mom's house after his passing, and was instrumental in keeping the glass intact there. If I remember correctly, the secretary was off limits to us kids for everything including hard glances. The angel-guarded glass survived the generations perfectly.

Somehow, over the years, the secretary became old-fashioned in Mom's eyes. We think that her state of mind changed with age and illness, and eventually she painted the thing. Painting the secretary was equivalent to painting the family dog or one of the grandchildren, but, proving how ill she was, she did it, using some incredibly durable cream-colored paint that was evidently baked on according to NASA specifications.

My sister inherited the secretary. When she and her husband retired to Leech Lake, she determined that it wouldn't fit in her house, so she offered it to me. I remembered it as that dark oak beauty with a mirror on top and that angel-protected curved glass front. Then she showed it to me. Before I had a chance to holler at her for desecrating a family monument, she said she regretted what Mom had done to it, announcing that she had no intention of refinishing anything like that, and had trouble even finishing a beer. My memories of the dark oak beauty were replaced by the reality of a mirrorless yellowing relic.

We took the secretary home fifty miles in the back of a pick-up, bound up and padded as though there were no angel guarding it at all. Getting rid of it was unthinkable considering its history.

My adoring wife chose to put up with it in our house for a time, but began hinting at a refinishing job. She'd hint with little comments such as, "When are you going to refinish that thing?" As a result I've been taking pieces of the secretary to the basement and trying to chisel off the painted finish. It's one of those nagging jobs that requires diligence and good fingernails and scrapers and a half dozen toothbrushes. When I announce that I'm going to the basement to strip the secretary, she no longer blanches and gives me the fish-eye. It's still fun to say that to others, though.

I practiced stripping a dresser at our daughter's house with good results, and for my purposes that makes me an expert. I've tried three or four kinds of finish removers so far, ranging from really thin stuff that you could drink, to really thick stuff that peels the skin off your hands. My work so far has resulted in refinished doors and drawers that prove we were right in not letting the thing escape to some antique shop. The cracking veneer under the paint proved to be cracking paint and no veneer, only solid oak. The curved-glass door survived refinishing and is beautiful, as you would expect an angel-guarded door to be.

Mom's paint job would have been a thing to admire, if it had only been on a Model A or the front door. The cabinet, outside and inside, is still cream colored. If I can stay retired and don't have to spend more time recovering from this summer's rains, it will return to its old oak glory. Somehow I will persevere. It will be refinished. If Churchill could get England through the blitz, I can get that old secretary through a refinishing job.

It won't be easy, though. I hope the guardian angel of the curved glass door can stick it out as well. He's had a rough tenure.

The Retiree—September, 2002—Trip

While crossing Idaho it occurred to me that our family's lives would be a whole lot simpler if we just had more compliant and maybe a little dumber children; kids who'd get a routine job in a factory and plug away until retirement. Simpler, but not as interesting. Unfortunately we didn't have kids whose goal was to make life simpler. One is preparing to move with her family to the Caribbean, and the other is arranging for a year in Germany.

As I write this, we are careering down a Montana mountain, heading for home via half-a-thousand miles of prairie. We just spent a week babysitting three small grandchildren and another week helping to strip a house for an international move. For three days we supervised a garage sale of gargantuan proportions. We offered for sale things like onesies, down jackets, tire chains, dressers, a guinea pig, bicycles, ski boots, a degausser, paint, a top rack, and chain oil. We collected for storage two cradles, a dog, a phonograph, an antique chair, stuffed animals, a picnic basket, my high chair, and a few hundred pounds of odds and ends. All are in our thirteen-year-old Bronco.

The dog is at eight on a ten-point confusion scale. She hasn't eaten for two days and shows no interest in urinating, both good properties for a touring dog. She misses her kids but would have a problem surviving the required six-month quarantine period for St. Lucia. Currently she's riding backwards behind the seat, staring at the cargo.

Well-wishers stopped by our kids' Boise house in bewildering profusion, rendering any attempts at organization futile. One night at about nine there were twelve people in the house, and two of the family members weren't even home. We tried driving the intruders off with a stick, the firearms already having been moved to Colorado, but by then we were so weak that we only succeeded in starting a hockey game in the dining room. One of the hockey sticks sold the next day for about half its fair value, eliminating any chance for the losing team to even the score.

There's a chance that the family's remaining furniture will be trucked to San Francisco and shipped by train to Miami where it will be put on a boat for St. Lucia. Or it may be trucked to Miami directly. Or it may be lost in transit, that being the most likely scenario.

We are looking for a language tape in Patois or French Creole. These two are the same language, evidently, and neither one is edible, contrary to my initial thought. English is the official language down there, but of course nobody uses it.

Roads on the island are miniscule and dirt and generally pasted on the side of a mountain. The son-in-law just bought a used Suburban. To use that vehicle on St. Lucia, he'd have to go offshore to turn around. City streets, according to the pictures we've seen, won't handle anything over four feet wide. The Suburban is necessary here and absurd there.

Well, finally I'm finishing this article at home. The old Bronco made it all the way back, and so did the dog. The stuff to be stored is put away in our shed. Given all we've been through I can offer this advice: Introduce your kids to some nice factory owner and burn all his or her books. The headaches you save may be your own.

The Retiree—October, 2002—Reunion

"Hi—I'm Bernice McWhittle-Dorsey (not her real name, I hope), and I'll be your waitress, or waitron, if there are any politically correct people among you," said the charming server with the genuine smile. We'd just begun another of those family outings at a smallish restaurant in a second-ring, not second-rate, suburb of The Big City. The cause for celebration this time was the imminent departure for the Caribbean of our lovely daughter and the family she's accumulated over the past eight years or so.

In attendance were our son-in-law's sister's Wisconsin family, our son and his family, some cousins of theirs, an uncle, a bunch of girl-kids, and after a great deal of badgering and persistence, Great-Grandma, age 91. There may have been a few non-relatives among the final 22 billed people, but after an hour or so nobody cared.

It being Sunday afternoon, nobody got in the bag or under the table, but alcohol is not required for the group. Half an hour into the lunch, everyone not in our group had left the restaurant, including all the help except Bernice McWhittle-Dorsey. In that half hour, Bernice McWhittle-Dorsey's genuine smile had begun to look a little plastic.

"One check all right with you?" said Bernice McWhittle-Dorsey. "One per family, if you don't mind," said a chorus of voices. "I'll start here," Bernice McWhittle-Dorsey said cheerily. What'll you have?"

"Burger for me, two coffees, pancakes for Dolores here, and see what the kid in the pink and the one wiping her nose on the tablecloth will have," said the guy in the sweatshirt who'd just come from church dressed that way but that's all right, at least he went to church.

Climbing back over the kiddy seat, one blanket, and a walker, Bernice McWhittle-Dorsey, still smiling gamely, continued. "How about you?"

"Chicken basket, and whatever my husband wants. He's in the ill-fitting brown suit. Get the girl in the hat and the one in the blue leotard over there under the coffee maker, too."

Bernice McWhittle-Dorsey continued around the tables, watching to see that Paul didn't order twice and that everyone got billed at least once. Her by-now painted-on smile pulled her off towards the kitchen, followed by shouts of "Make that two Pepsis" and "I want water, too."

"Who didn't come? Where's Walt? Whatever happened to Dot and Millie? How about Fern?" called a voice from near the window.

"Sick, not invited, sick too, and who's Fern?" replied some unidentified voice near the wall.

"Fern's your great-aunt, you twit, and anyway you were supposed to invite Walt," said one of the organizers, if indeed anything had been organized, either by the family or the restaurant.

Banter continued apace for an hour. When I stepped outside to escort Great-Grandma to the car, the door was locked behind me. I suspect that Bernice McWhittle-Dorsey had enough and was seeking any possible way of minimizing damage to her employer and her psyche. I'm not sure, but I think I heard a maniacal laugh behind the curtained glass. We waited in the car, quietly, trying to discern the level of damage that had been done to the family by one more get-together.

Since our son leaves shortly for military reserve activation, we expect a repeat of this event. We will try to spare the second-ring suburb a repeat of the event, and trust that Bernice McWhittle-Dorsey will recover with no permanent damage.

The Retiree—October, 2002—Colors

BP, with a conscious disregard for the norm, rebelled against the concept of "green means diesel" so I determined to find out what was going on. Naturally, I turned to Brisbane McFogarland, the internationally renowned discerner of colors, and the person most likely to be upset by infractions of this sort.

"Mr. McFogarland," I asked, "Isn't the use of green for gasoline hose nozzles a deliberate and irresponsible violation of the rules of color that are held dear by so many of us nearly normal citizens? And isn't it your prerogative to make such changes, and to supervise and coordinate things like this? How many diesel tanks have to be filled with gasoline before something is done?"

"Call me Brisbane," said Mr. McFogarland. "Yes, you are correct. I am the principal architect of color designations in the western world. I am upset with BP and their disregard for Rule 21.6.4 Paragraph 8, specifically requiring the use of green for diesel."

"Fortunately I do not have a diesel vehicle," I said, "but I have put 89-octane gas in a car that would run on 87-octane, just because I didn't trust the green nozzle."

"Exactly. Can't trust those British at BP. Brits even painted battleships with straight line camouflage in the War to End All Wars."

Brisbane McFogarland was becoming agitated. He continued. "The McFogarlands have for many generations been the people in charge of color discernment. Egil McFogarland painted the first fire engine red, and his brother Cecil used orange on a road grader. The rest is history. We're not fond of publicity, you understand, but we do take a certain pride in our responsibilities, and we view such violations with alarm."

"I understand. It's the blue for skim and green for one-percent thing."

"And red for whole. You know that. Everyone knows that. Then, some idiot with complete disregard for tradition comes up with a yellow one-percent, and all hell breaks loose." Brisbane McFogarland's veins were standing out on his forehead. "It's amazing that I don't lose my mind sometimes."

"Green for decaf, right?"

"Green when in bean form, and orange when brewed and in a pot. Don't get them mixed up. Black for caffeine. Never change that." He was sweating profusely. "It's seldom violated, although I know for a fact that some people use decaf in the caffeinated pots in unscrupulous restaurants when they run out. We prosecute people for that," said Brisbane with a snarl.

"Really? Were there always such stringent regulations? Do violations cause problems?"

Brisbane McFogarland shouted, "You've seen the problems that came about when shotgun shells became something other than red. We finally threw up our hands and just gave up on that one. The pheasant population hasn't been the same since. And no more passenger pigeons. When's the last time you saw a penguin in the wild around here?"

"Penguin?"

"Maybe I overstated the problem a little there, but mark my words, the world will not be the same if such things aren't policed. Green for regular, indeed. Chartreuse fire engines. The world is going to regret those things, I've no doubt."

Brisbane McFogarland wandered off, muttering to himself. He climbed into a black 1939 Ford and drove slowly away, sideswiping the green BP regular pump on his way out.

I went into the station to pick up some milk. Blue cap. And butter in a yellow carton. And some brown-packaged chocolate. Some things shouldn't change.

The Retiree—October, 2002—Institute

Awhile after my fifth retirement, deep in a malaise after an operation, unable to do any heavy work, and bored, I invented the Maple Lake Institute. This organization was (and is, come to think of it) dedicated to the investigation of a variety of causes that nobody else gives a rip about. Its exalted title allows me to write the most outrageous things without bringing any sort of criticism on me, and I can call on any number of seemingly knowledgeable authorities who may or may not exist. What a deal. I should have thought of it long ago.

The Maple Lake Institute is currently investigating ads for candidates for election. Other people analyzed things like this, too, but they are inhibited by things like truth and right and dedication. None of these bothers me.

Here are transcripts of ads gleaned from the latest election campaign. I have, or rather the Institute has, put the various statements together in a sort of montage of arguments.

"Politician A voted against children and motherhood and the flag, and our candidate is so repelled by his actions that he actually puked."

"Candidate B supported theft from old people and wants Social Security to be converted to payments to the drug companies, even though he hasn't been in the legislature and knows nothing about government."

"Oh yeah? Candidate B supports money for schools from the Federal government, which everyone knows is free money that nobody pays for and if we don't get it, Alabama will, and besides Politician A wants to close all schools and burn the teachers at the stake."

"Bull hockey, you dip, Politician A wants schools on every corner with bonuses to teachers who actually show up, and if we don't pay for it now, we'll have to pay later."

"Well, Candidate B wants every kid to be all that he can be, and it all starts at home, so he will support supporting home."

"Candidate B is a big fat liar and he should be ashamed of himself for being a bigoted demoniacal monster who has dirty fingernails and bad breath!"

"Nyaah nyaah nyaah, you big naughty fat dummy! Go shape up and behave yourself!"

"You're not the boss of me! I can do anything I wanna!"

"Mom! He's calling me names! Take that, you jerk!"

"Ow! Why you moron! I oughtta…"

You get the idea. Our actual research at the Institute has shown that only four percent (4.12%) of voters were actually influenced by the ads for either party. Other statistics from the Maple Lake Institute's exhaustive study follow.

6.11% went to the refrigerator whenever an ad came on.

22.4% went to the bathroom.

16.6% slept.

91% had made up their minds before anything was done, using critical analysis methods such as who had the better hair, which voice caused a headache, who daddy voted for, which party had the best bean feed, and who didn't interrupt dinner with a phone call.

For my part, and the Maple Lake Institute's, we look forward to a peaceful winter devoid of ads. Look for the next Institute analysis. No telling what it will be about.

The Retiree—November, 2002—Reunion

Once again there was a meeting of some of the in-town inlaws and the out-of-town inlaws. The out-of-town inlaws usually make a farm trip out of it, and show up with a fifth-wheel full of cows or cow leavings. This procedure limits the places where we can visit. Places like the Marquette Inn in the Crystal Court are out. Neutral ground in Hutchinson was chosen.

This was a low-key session. We didn't pick on the waitress nearly as much as last time, and there was no store closing across the road to browse through, and there had been no new nieces or nephews or news since the last session. Our only source of confusion seemed to be names of shirt-tail relatives, and when one considers how family stories can become mixed up, maybe that's enough to chew on for one lunch. Here are a few quotes, jammed together in just the way the conversation was.

"DJ, or Cousin DJ? Is it the Librarian David you're talking about? And did you say 'Kim and Sue' or 'Tim and Sue?' Those are two different families, you know."

"Not Chuck and Sue? Why does everyone marry Sue?"

"They don't. Everyone at the lake married Carol."

"She had her teeth pulled so she'd be eligible for a kidney transplant."

"Pulled her teeth? Where are they putting that kidney anyway?"

"That makes sense. My dentist gives me antibiotics for my knee."

"Lupus or loopy? Did it leave a butterfly stain on the face?"

"What was a butterfly doing in the doctor's office?"

"Remember that family in Delft, I think, who lost someone in a grain bin a couple years ago? Didn't get him out until the grain prices went up."

"Got new shoes for the artificial turf, and then they didn't put him in the game, but he's only a freshman. I hope his feet don't grow much."

"Team's losing a buncha seniors. He don't have to worry about artificial turf. I hope the shoes are good in cow turf. Yes I said turf."

"Rented by a Laotian named La. La the Laotian. Has family named Do, Re, Mi, Fa…"

"Someone said he bought a Spanish SUV, I think, something called a Chev Taco."

"Roxanne or Eleanor, in Lake Havasu or Roseburg, had someone in an urn."

"That wasn't the same family. That was Candy's mom. They waited three years to pot her, or was it plant her. Buried her with the cardboard box. And it wasn't Roxanne in Roseburg. I think it was either that divorced cousin of theirs or Menno."

"What's a Menno? Oh, I remember from the reunion, DJ's adopted cousin's husband who didn't come, along with Ed and what was his name with the rented Lincoln?"

"Which DJ? You're mixed up with Karschnik or Cody or Kremin or Kremlin or something."

"Jack's taller than the Paddington Bear now, but you probably haven't seen the Paddington Bear because you can't get that fifth-wheel full of cows into the ramp."

"We don't take that cow trailer everywhere, you know. Just here to lunch once in awhile."

"And church. Of course you had all those kids visiting and no room inside the pickup."

There was more, of course, involving grain and how to get the smell out of the Sunday School and where to get a kidney and who still owed a tip, but we had to quit. At least, that's what the waitress said. With holidays rampant, there's little chance of having to worry about answers to any questions that came up. We're all getting too old to remember what the questions were, anyway.

The Retiree—December, 2002—Dog

Our daughter's dog Lucky is spending an extended time, 5 or 6 years, with us as an unpaying boarder. The dog's family is out of the country and she (the dog) couldn't go along. Something about a passport.

Lucky has a few bad habits. One of these is a notion that cats and squirrels are inherently evil and she has been appointed an angel of death to rid the world of them.

Another bad habit is an inclination to roll in things. She could have selected oak leaves or grass or snow, which would have been only a minimal problem. Instead, she selected something else. Let's call them biscuits.

There are many creatures at the lake depositing biscuits in various forms. The aforementioned squirrels and cats do so. We've seen some raccoon biscuits, and of course dog biscuits. Occasionally there are horse biscuits on the road. All these biscuits are attractive to the dog. Lucky's favorite biscuits, however, are from cows.

Cow pies---or biscuits---have been generously spread on a bean field behind our place. Spreading cow biscuits on the field is a tradition dating back many years, and is one which we dare not suggest changing. Unfortunately, this very tradition is at the seat of Lucky's compulsion. Because of this tradition, Lucky has been thrown in a cold lake 3 times, has had 3 dry-shampoo baths, and has been thoroughly (emphasis on roughly) bathed 4 times, all within a month's time.

We recently visited the dairy farm of a relative with Lucky in tow. She was literally in tow, as we didn't dare let her off the leash. On one of her walks, I decided to show her the source of her favorite biscuits. There were about 20 heifers in an enclosure, and the smell of fresh biscuits was attractive to Lucky.

One heifer was at the fence, and wanted to meet Lucky. I let them go nose to nose for a few minutes, while Lucky raised the hair on her back and tried to look like she weighed 700 pounds, too. Lucky put on a good show of bravery and proved to herself that she could master the situation. She could show that biscuit-maker who was boss, all right.

She showed them until the rest of the herd got curious and came over to the fence. One look at 7 or 8 tons of beef changed her mind. She looked at me, and her eyes said "I think I'd like to go back to the house now. Right now. Immediately."

We let Lucky run today. She came home with no biscuit smell on her back.

Maybe the problem has been solved. It would be nice if we could find a fenced-in area where there are herds of squirrels, cats, horses, and raccoons. Going nose-to-nose with a battle group of hostile cats or violent raccoons would do a lot to straighten out her penchant for rolling, I'm sure. There's nothing like fear to change a habit.

But there's that memory thing. Memory is a problem for lots of us. For Lucky, it seems to be particularly problematic. It's entirely possible that, deep down in that tiny brain of hers, there's a circuit that is hard-wired to roll in biscuits. The switch has been thrown on cows for now, but it just may be on a timer, and like a yard light, pretty soon it will go snap and we'll be back in the dog-washing business.

We'd be grateful for suggestions. Non-destructive solutions are preferred. We have only about 5 or 6 years left to worry about her.

The Retiree—September, 2002—Dog

Everybody with a dog has cute stories about the dog, such as what he rolled in, what he ate, where he threw up, who shot at him and why, what they stepped in and where it was, and so forth. I'm no different. Here are mine.

We put down our last dog in Connecticut during my fourth retirement, when she just got too old to function any more. The dog before that lasted for a coon's age as well. Two dogs got us through thirty years of marriage, counting a short break after year fourteen. After that we said no more dogs, we've had enough, we get too attached.

Then our daughter moved to St. Lucia and didn't want to put their dog through a six-month quarantine, so we have a dog again.

She's a good dog, as dogs go. She's Australian Shepherd and can jump like a kangaroo but doesn't have a six-foot fence to peek over any more, so she doesn't have to jump. She can corner like a Ferrari but now the landscape is wide open and she doesn't have to turn. She had two little girls and a baby boy to play with, but now she has two seniors so she doesn't have to play. She loves to wade in rivers, but shows little interest in our calm lake so she doesn't have to wade. We think she's bored.

Relatives with a dairy farm want to put her to work. She'd do a good job, probably, but she's slightly disadvantaged in that she's never seen a cow. Or a sheep. The most herding she's done, besides the kids, was twenty minutes trying to herd her cousin-dog, a Labrador. We told her that she's a working dog, and a Lab is a sporting dog, and sporting dogs don't like to be herded. The Lab told her so, too.

She's an indoor dog now, used to mild Idaho desert winters. We're not sure how she'd handle a light coating of cow manure, although she does enjoy rolling in some very unsavory things. The longer she hangs around the more she likes it here, and we haven't found a reason yet to regret her presence. She makes a fuss when strangers come around, and doesn't make a fuss when we tell her not to, and she comes when called. Although we have tried to find reasons to exile her to the farm, there are few.

Currently the dog is concerned with heating system cold-air returns. She's often found peering down them, and we have no idea why. I opened one register for her, and she cleaned it out with her muzzle. She had to be pulled out or she would have spent the day there, head under the floor. She's also a flycatcher. And beecatcher. She eats them. Maybe bees are sweet. I'll never know.

If only she'd rip an escaped convict to shreds, or save a drowning neighbor, or bring us the mail, or maybe put out a house fire, we would have a good solid reason to keep her. Or if she'd eat the Schwan's man, or barf on the carpet, or dig holes in the garden, we'd have a good reason to put her in cow country. So far, my wife and I just look at each other, and maybe let her chase a tennis ball or pull on a rope, and ponder her fate. Working dog or entertainment?

It isn't easy keeping a dog. But then, it isn't very hard, either.

The Retiree—December, 2002— Christmas Past

Holidays are but a memory again. Just saying that brings back memories of the past, and Christmas at Grandma's house. Retirees have an advantage over working folk in that their memories become more malleable over time, and can include pleasant events that maybe weren't quite as pleasant when they happened, such as the times when all the uncles disappeared into the basement where Grandpa kept the bourbon.

I recall, only vaguely (which allows a little artistic license), all the Christmases past, when the family dressed in native costumes and sang carols in the languages of the Old Country, wherever that was. I can still see Mom dressed in her WWII artillery uniform, full field pack on her back, blasting out some Mozart opera completely off key. My sister doesn't remember that one. And Dad, in a dashiki and Australian campaign hat, dancing an Irish jig on the coffee table. She denies that one, too.

The aunts would assemble around the piano in a chorus, singing German or Lithuanian carols in Norwegian or Swedish, alternating languages individually verse by verse. One would be wearing lederhosen with a Slovak embroidered blouse; another would have a cowboy shirt and chaps; another a ballerina skirt and wool hunting socks. It was lovely.

After dinner, the uncles would sit on the couch and exchange hunting stories until one by one they fell sound asleep, unless they retreated to the basement as mentioned before. We cousins always looked forward to their becoming comatose, as we could then go outside and slide down the hill on cardboard in our Sunday best until our long underwear froze to our shoes and our fingers got numb.

The women would gather in the kitchen, trying to bamboozle Grandma into giving up her recipe for putukagu or something like that, and chipping lutefisk residue off the kitchen windows. Their shrill arguments seldom developed into fighting. Since smoking wasn't anathema at that time except with Grandma, a few of them would sneak off to the upstairs bathroom where they would open the window and smoke until the neighbors called the fire department.

Dinner included lefse, lutefisk, blood sausage, herring, and a number of edibles for those of us who grew up too late to appreciate that other junk. Everyone ate heartily but enough food remained to take care of supper and for Grandma to send a little to Great-uncle Ole down in a flophouse on Hennepin, if he should show up, which she didn't expect anyway. He could get a better dinner at the Salvation Army, and he wouldn't have to walk four miles to get it.

New Year's Eve was quite low key, with only one or two aunt-uncle pairs coming over to our house. Nobody could afford to go out anywhere. The adults would drink cheap whiskey and 7-Up and play cards and smoke until all the towels stunk. We kids would listen to midnight coming across the world on the radio. London, Rio, Havana, New York. Guy Lombardo would make our stomachs hurt. Maybe the 7-Up and cookies helped do that. Dad would tell about how, when he was a kid, they would watch the old guy down on Second Street kick the calendar out his door at midnight, making us think our celebration was pretty wild in comparison. At midnight in the Central Time Zone, we'd all open the doors and holler and then we'd go to bed. Come to think of it, that's about all we do now.

Maybe by next year I can embellish my memory a little more. My wild times were all in the big city. If anyone has memories of how things went out in the country, let me know. It all sounds pretty good from my perspective.

Young folks just don't know how to have a good time any more.

The Retiree—Memorial Day

Memorial Day. A time for a little introspection, a little thought about current times, about the past, about our future, and about our hearts.

It was a Sunday afternoon in March 1992. I was in Germany on business, in Goettingen, a university town, waiting for it to stop raining. It rained almost all the time in Germany in that early spring. When it did stop raining and the sun came out, it was time for a walk.

A few blocks from the Ropeter Hotel, where I was staying, there was a cemetery, with an entrance just off busy Kasseler Landstrasse. I turned through the open wrought-iron gate and went in. There were cobblestone pathways, a stone wall, manicured grass, trees, and in its own little grassy area, a huge ancient iron pump to water the flowers. In a corner, by the wall opposite the pump, was the Meier family plot.

Headstones showed that Grandfather and Grandmother Meier were there. So was Father and, much later, Mother. Aunts, uncles. And a son. Friedrich; 1920—1943 it said. Leutnant. A soldier.

Above the family plot, a big old tree was awaiting its spring leaves. It was symmetrical except for one missing branch, and through that opening, the sun was shining more brightly on Friedrich's stone than on the rest. What had happened to the branch was not apparent. Lightning? Wind? Disease? No nests there, no leaves, no seeds.

It had been forty-nine years since they buried Leutnant Friedrich

Meier there. Mother had stood where I stood, and how she must have cried. Military funeral. A squad fired their Mausers there. A flag was folded and given to Mother. Which flag? The Iron Cross? Swastika? No one would show those flags now.

How did Friedrich fall? At Leningrad or Kursk? A bullet from the French Resistance? Prisoner? Hero of the Third Reich, or traitor? Slowly, from disease? Face down in the sands of Tunisia? Did he come from Georg August Universitat, ready to conquer, eager for battle, Deutschland uber Alles? Or was he conscripted? No widow, no children. No memories, either, by now, after almost half a century in the ground. Duty, honor, country...

Does it matter? After all, Friedrich is gone, just like the branch.

Yes, it matters. The Meier family, like the tree, lost a branch. Healed over now, but what would have grown there? A wife? Children? Doctor, statesman, mechanic, fool? We'll never know. But we need to care, we must care, about war, cemeteries, stones, branches, trees, memories, hopes, dreams unfulfilled.

As I stood there by Leutnant Friedrich Meier's grave, it clouded up again, and a drizzle started. I hurried back through the gate, back to Kasseler Landstrasse, to the hotel, thinking about the rain, about the the war, and about the Meier family, about the tree without the branch. Thinking that maybe Memorial Day isn't only for heroes or winners. Maybe it's also for the fearful, for foot soldiers and clerks, for nurses and cooks. Maybe it's for conscripts, for guardsmen and reservists who weren't called up, for those who just kept their heads down and waited for it all to end. Maybe it's for traitors and cowards as well, for those who wouldn't have been traitors and cowards without a war. Maybe it's for enemies too, who, misguided or not, gave the supreme sacrifice for a country in which they believed and wanted to protect.

Memorial Day is for our past, and, most of all, it's for our future. We must not forget. God help us. Take off your hat, and bow your head.

And have a nice Memorial Day.

The Retiree—January, 2003—Messaging

A lot of activities require outside communication when a retiree goes to church in a suburb of the Big City, and when the children are out of the country. We have advanced into the Realm of High Technology with some of our messages. Not only do we e-mail to beat the dickens, we are also connected to exotic places such as St. Lucia and Minneapolis by computer, through which we can get voices and pictures of a chosen few people at particular times when we are all accidentally on line at the same time.

Theoretically we save money by using the computer to communicate. The theory assumes that we can find each other at opportune times. So far, we have missed each other about fifteen times for each one that we connected. Our computer bill has doubled. So has that of our daughter. They get you on both ends when you use a computer.

Fortunately, the computer process allows for sending and receiving typed notes, in case the object of our communication is busy communicating with someone in Colorado or Wisconsin, for example. When we log on, we can see who is on line, and if no one is there, we leave a note.

Our register of notes reads something like this:

"Missed you. Will try at 10 (12 your time)."

"Ha! We looked and you weren't there. Try at 6 (4 your time).

"Where were you? Try again at 8 (10 there)."

"See you tomorrow. Make that the day after as we are going away. How's the dog?"

"Where were you? Try noon here. Dog's fine, picture in e-mail. Do you want the snail-mail sent soon?"

"You were not there. Send the mail; we've got plenty snails. Dog looks good."

"DING" (That's what happens when you connect, or at least when someone thinks you did.)

Most of the conversation concerns getting the grandchildren to talk or the dog to bark. That's the way we used to do it on the telephone, too, so progress hasn't gone backwards, but hasn't advanced perceptibly, either, except that now they can see the dog bark.

One concern with the computer is that someone else controls the phone line. If someone in Annandale or Castries or Miami or Chicago or Tulsa or Winnemucca or heaven knows where flips a switch, you may get the Blue Screen of Death and your conversation ends. Or if a cloud appears over Martinique or lightning strikes in Omaha, bingo, you start over. Or if the dog kicks out the plug, down she goes and when you power up that insulting Microsoft message says don't shut the thing down that way again, you dunce.

My grandparents came over from the Old Country. They said good-bye to the old folks and maybe they wrote letters, maybe not. No telephone, no computer, no web cam.

We couldn't operate that way, and don't have to. Call it civilization or progress or persistence, we now take it for granted that we will be able to talk to our grandkids, and see them, however jerkily, from time to time. On occasion, we pick up the phone, dial 39 digits, and get an answering machine to absorb our digital message. If we do connect, we can actually hear the dollars we spent on the phone card being sucked into the Caribbean.

It's better than getting a ride in a buckboard to the station, riding a steam train for three days to a dingy port, taking a steamship for two weeks to another dingy port, riding another train for a few hours, and walking ten kilometers uphill to find out no one's home. We do have it pretty good, after all.

But there's still the Blue Screen of Death, and Microsoft's insulting messages. Grandpa never had to deal with that.

The Retiree—February, 2003—Trip

Retirees have to take trips. It's part of the obligation of a retiree. We recognize our duty so we took another trip. Florida again, to Barefoot Bay, a community of people wearing double-knit slacks and baseball caps and walking slowly around the block.

A storm moved ahead of us but Minnesotans are not discouraged by bad weather. We avoided Chicago, making travel easier, but to do so we had to take I-39 from Beloit to Normal. That stretch is the most desolate road in the known universe even though thousands of cars traverse it every day. The road has one rest stop and a bunch of towns with no restaurants ten miles from the interstate. Beloit has half a buck of tolls, its only claim to fame, and Normal is a ball spot on the big pool table called the American Prairie. I kept looking for six pockets and an immense cue ball. Dull doesn't begin to describe the drive. The highest point in Illinois is along I-39, and it's an overpass.

We stopped in South Carolina, our home for five years. Retirees look for free stuff, so we visited friends for food and a couple night's rest. We promised them the same when they visit us up here, but when they visited us last we took them to Duluth—50 degrees and raining—so it may be awhile.

When we lived in Columbia we had record heat, and when we moved to Hartford we had record snow, so it didn't surprise us to find record cold in Florida. A manatee watcher in Fort Pierce told us he'd seen snowflakes, and a guy on TV was making snow angels on the grass in Orlando even though no snow could be seen.

Florida is like a chocolate-covered cherry. The chocolate around the outside is all Yankees, and the cherry in the center is solid South. The beaches are thick with chocolate. In Barefoot Bay the chocolate is thin. When we got a new starter put in the car, we found a shop full of whatever non-Floridians call the natives. That could be rednecks, crackers, good ol' boys, or something less complimentary. Whatever they are, they are entertaining. Beck, the mechanic, is a type-A personality. His assistant dropped us at a restaurant to wait out the repair. His first attempt at using a car was thwarted when the owner came out and drove away. We were loaded into another car, where the assistant said that to ask Beck a question after his morning coffee and a Coke, you had to chase him down and pin him to the wall. Barefootbayitans drop off cars to repair things that don't necessarily need repair. They may leave a car for a few days because the washer is out of fluid. Beck takes checks, cash, and any plastic, and he's looking for a way to take food stamps.

The car needed a part, so we took a walk. Our walk took us to the library where the computer was down and then to Big Roman's, which was far out of the cherry center and deeply into the chocolate. Big Roman had a Jersey accent. He sold pizza and soda complete with insults. By the time we'd finished our lunch, he'd called my wife's diamond ring glass, sold fifteen feet of sausage to a New Yorker who was going to have a party, and dealt loudly and rudely with a salesman. The salesman didn't care, though. He sounded like a New Yorker himself, and said Big Roman would buy anything if he hung around long enough. By the time our car was ready Big Roman had bought two lamps and was looking at a backpack and a picnic set. We enjoyed the show, and told Big Roman he should have a cover charge.

The beach was cold. Nights were frosty. Friends were warm, though, and Beck and Big Roman and Nellie—some day I'll tell about Nellie— gave us all the entertainment we could handle. Try Barefoot Bay some time. Especially if your car needs work.

The Retiree—February, 2003—Sliding

The grandgirls were here overnight. To entertain them we made a sliding trail down our modest hill to the lake. The girls thought the slide was great, which was gratifying to one who dragged a scoop down the hill to make the trail. A couple sled runs provided a good track for the young, inexperienced sledders, and it made Grandpa puff a little. No, a lot.

Modern sliding has progressed greatly from the days of the Flexible Flyer. But it isn't the same as back when I did my sliding. My memories may be colored by the passage of time, but I'm sure I don't exaggerate much when I recall those great sliding days.

My grandparents lived on the Fourth Street side of the Sixth Street Hill, fabled in story and song all over North Minneapolis, and I lived on the flat of Sixth Street above the hill. I spent every day of my winters on that hill. The temperature was always below zero, the wind always blew down the hill, and it snowed from early December until late March.

There was no alley between Fourth and Sixth (there was no Fifth) on the hill. Nobody lived in that part of the block. The 6th Street side was wooded, and the sliding hill was on open land towards Fourth Street. Our main slide went from the hilltop to the street and permitted speeds of maybe 100 miles per hour. Midway was a jump about five feet high. We stopped by hitting cinders in the street (forbidden by parents), bare sidewalk (shoveled by Grandpa), an elm tree on the boulevard, or Grandpa's garden fence. Sometimes we ran into a drift by Mrs. Dolander's house, and tried to get out before she yelled at us.

Across the alley was an iced slide maintained by the Sixth Street Gang. Trespassing on their slide was punishable by death, so we rarely went there. It had mounds similar to San Fransisco cross-streets. Speeds of up to 200 miles per hour could be attained, with jumps of fifty feet or so. We tried it a few times each year, and used the death threat as an excuse to stay away, although the real reason was that we didn't want broken bones.

Our sliding was done on sleds with steel runners, one of which was always loose. We used various launching techniques from bellyflopping after a short run to getting pushed by unfriendly kids who wanted to see the sound barrier broken. We frequently lost our buttons sliding over the front of the sled when we stopped on the sidewalk.

Mom dressed us in heavy socks, shoes, wool socks over the shoes, and overshoes over the socks. We wore long underwear, corduroy pants, snow pants, shirt, sweater, heavy jacket, a scarf tied around the upturned collar, a leather flying helmet with sheepskin lining, and Norwegian mittens knit by Grandma. It was time to go home when all our zippers had developed clods of ice, the scarf had become untied or lost, and we couldn't feel anything in our feet.

Usually there was a cadre of dogs on the hill with the avowed purpose of tearing off the feet of sledders. After awhile the dogs' feet got cold too, and once everyone's overshoe buckles had been pulled off, they would go home.

I'd find my way home in the semidarkness once most of the other kids had left. In an emergency I could go to Grandma's house if I felt like I'd lose a foot or my nose to the cold, or if my dog became unable to walk from exertion or cold. That extended my sliding time. Grandma had cookies, although eating wasn't foremost in the mind of one who had just broken the sound barrier on the Sixth Street Hill.

Kids just don't know what sliding is any more.

The Retiree—February, 2003—Colds

Baybe you doticed. I'be dot a code. (snort) I think it cabe od (sniff) whed we had the grandgirls over. Every tibe we do anythigg with children, I get a code. For the first tibe in about a decade I got a flu shot, so I know it isn't da flu. (sneeze) If I thought it was da flu I would sue da Center for Disease Control. (sneeze) (cough cough)

Durig by third retirebent (snort) ad all da while I was workig before dat I dever had a code. (sneeze). We didn't see the grandgirls as often den. I deterbined den dat we don't deed sdow, as working dere and that third retirebent were in South Carolina. (sneeze) We had do salt on da roads, ad soil was pure sand, so cars and entry halls were always clean. (sneeze) (cough) But da accumulated effect of dot beig able to afford food and the government's restrictions on IRAs (sniff) ad da fact dat oatmeal cookies stayed soggy in da humidity sent us to the sdow belt agaid, (sniff) where we were once bore exposed to (sneeze) (cough) (snort) codes.

Dis tibe whed I gor my code I had a dental appoitmedt. I called dem to see if dey would still serve be because I didn't want to sdeeze a pick across da roob ad impale sobebody. Dey said dey had masks ad gloves ad probably chest protectors so cobe alog. (sneeze) (cough) Rats.

Evidently I don't cough or sneeze when I am flat on my back, which is how by dentist works. Me, dat is, not da dentist or da dentist gum-massager tooth cleaner persod. (sneeze) The appoitmedt went as well as could be expected, ad I went home to bore sdeezig ad coughing. (sneeze) Dow both be ad by wife habe codes, ad she admits to beig biserable just like be. (cough) Dere's sobethig cobfortig about dat, aldough I don't like to see her biserable.

Dere is a good side to dis, dough. We are pladdig anoder trip. (sneeze) Dis tibe we will be a logg tibe on an airplade, ad by den we both should be recovered. We won't be susceptible to codes for a few weeks den. Goig up in da air is hard on ears adyway, eben widout a code. (sneeze) (cough)

I hate it when I bleed frob da ears.

The Retiree—March, 2003—Nellie

Nellie is a fine retired Irish lady, a widow with a ready smile and a most cheerful outlook. She lives next door to the "manufactured home" that we rented in Florida in January. For the past two winters we've spent some time there. Nellie was mentioned to us frequently as someone we had to meet by our friends in that faraway neighborhood, but we hadn't met her until this trip. This time, we found out why we needed to visit with her.

Back in 1952, Nellie came over from Ireland. It wasn't easy for her. Back then, people didn't just walk into the country. A couple illnesses resulted in setbacks and denials of entry, but she didn't give up. When she did finally get into the country, to New York, she brought along an independent attitude and a charming brogue, neither of which has been lost over the years. They both suit her well. She married, became a citizen, and held a responsible job at a university. Nellie must have been a beautiful girl then, as she is still quite striking for someone well into her seventies. She wouldn't mind my giving her age, but I'm sure she'd have a comment or two.

Most of the manufactured homes in Barefoot Bay are functional, inexpensive and predictably laid out. There's a big sedan parked outside each of them with a New Jersey or Ohio or Minnesota license on it. Households are modest with all the good stuff having been left up North. Not so with Nellie. Her house was built in a factory, but outfitted especially for her, and her old spotlessly clean Chev has a Florida plate. She's got a carafe of wine or maybe two waiting for visitors, with some brie or cheddar and crackers ready. The furnishings are exactly right for her, and the place looks like a magazine spread.

When one of her comrades needs a trip to the doctor or the drug store, Nellie's the one who takes her there. When someone goes back up North for a visit, Nellie watches the house. When frost is predicted, those are Nellie's pillowcases covering the flowers. Nellie brought us her newspaper every morning after she'd finished with it. If we weren't there, she bagged it and hung it from the doorknob.

Whenever we go on a trip I find it easy to comment on strange people or unusual places we've encountered. I suppose the strange people comment similarly on me. There are always enough weird things that happen on our trips to make a column of a few hundred words. It's nice once in awhile, though, just to recall that there are still charming, helpful, involved people out there, doing good things for others, and smiling all the while.

Nellie readily told us about her family in Ireland, the culture there, how people thought about her and the U.S.A. She invited us in for wine and cheese. She came over to talk (and talk and talk) to us before we left. She shared memories of her time in New York City. She made us feel like old friends from the very start. Nellie has a knack for that.

Some people seem to retire right, and keep busy doing things that are worth while. It's comforting to find someone like that. Knowing there are still such people around makes it easier for me to continue to be a surly, abusive, cantankerous, uncooperative curmudgeon.

The Retiree—March 11, 2003—Belle

Belle set a new record the other day. Twenty laps around the dining room table. Lucky matched it, with an added trip around the rocking chair every five or six laps. Belle was carrying a length of rope, which always starts the parade around the table, but after two or three laps, the significance of the rope was forgotten and the laps were run for their own sake. Trips begin slow, with speed increasing right up to the end. The previous lap record was 11, matched twice the following day. A new option was introduced after that first record; 6 counterclockwise and 5 clockwise laps. That made it evident that 11 was the magic number, but we found out later that it's not.

Once in awhile, when we're outside doing something besides watching the dogs, we let them run. Apologies to those people in Alexandria and Rochester who wonder what those zooming animals were that flashed through their yards. The two need substantial room to turn at the high speeds they attain. Fortunately they tend to zip through our yard from time to time, and they do respond to voice commands. However, at maximum speed, returning to the door takes a few minutes at best, and in the process they occasionally forget the commands.

When Belle came to visit Lucky, she remembered the rope-table game from her last time here. Belle's a Labrador, and Lucky's an Australian Shepherd. We are taking care of Belle for a couple weeks and Lucky for five or six years, to help our kids out while they wander around the world. We've found that having two big dogs is the same as having a dozen. There's a limited amount of room under one's feet, and two big dogs can fill it completely.

One night Belle determined that she needed to go out around 1:30 a.m. and of course she needed breakfast at about six. Lucky sleeps late and has a bladder the size of Toronto, so we're not used to the interruptions. Both of them like to lick hands that are dangling off the bed, regardless of the hour, and they apparently wake each other up from time to time to perform licking duty. Oh, well, we can sleep later.

People with hard flooring shouldn't have dogs with claws. The noise is almost too much to bear. Tickticktickticktick all day long. Both dogs avoid carpeting, except when taking table laps. We have cut their claws before but to get them down to a quieter level would require surgery. We could use some of those booties that sled dogs wear, but after all, these aren't our dogs, and from time to time they do stop to sleep, so they can stay awake during the night.

Belle eats her food in one gulp, twice a day. Then she finds someone to burp at. Lucky eats daintily all day long, unless her cousin is visiting. Then she gulps it down and looks for the Lab's dish. They don't usually fight over food, thankfully, or we'd really have a problem. Once the two of them decided who was dominant, they decided not to contend for anything. Lucky's the dominant one. It's her house, Belle decided, and she's not a fighter.

We're not complaining. Not too much, anyway. The dogs need someone to take care of them, and they do entertain us. Watching the evening table laps is great fun, and the carpet should be able to take a little more of it. Stop over some night to watch the races. Don't forget to bring something to take the dog hair off your clothes.

The Retiree—March, 2003—Trip

Yes we did go on another trip and yes we are worn out and yes we had a good time and yes I do plan to bore everyone I can think of with all the details I can remember. The last ones involve security in Amsterdam. I suspect there are people in a waiting room in Amsterdam who have been there since they were young and are trying to get home to retire. Fortunately we were already retired.

Our tickets said be at the gate by 3 or we will put you in a Dutch prison for the rest of your miserable lives even though the plane won't leave until 4:30. When we got to the gate there were already 40 bewildered passengers in line, waiting for 8 or 10 uniformed rent-a-cops to ask silly questions. Maybe the questions weren't silly if everyone gave honest answers, but also maybe my parenthetical thoughts below were shared by others in that massive entourage. Here's part of what went on.

"How did you get to the airport?" (On one of your planes.) Flew in from Stuttgart.

"How did you get to that airplane?" (What difference does it make? After all, they frisked us in Stuttgart.) Our daughter-in-law brought us.

"How did she bring you?" In a car.

"Private car?" (No, lieutenant car.) Yes.

"Who packed your bags?" (The maid. You must know that everyone in Germany has a maid.) We did.

"Did you watch whoever packed your bags?" (I always watch the maid.) We did it alone.

"Have your bags been out of your possession?" (Yes, on your airplane.) No except once when I forgot one in a coffee shop a couple years ago.

"Today, have they been out of your possession?" (No sense of humor here. Out of our possession only when in your overhead bin.) No.

"Has anyone watched your carryon bags for you?" (Someone else did once when I went to get a longer fuse for the bomb.) No.

"Please proceed to the x-ray machine over there by those people who have been trained in the martial arts. Thank you." Okay, bitte bitte danke schoen.

"Put your bag, coat, shoes, belt and packages on the belt." (My pants are falling down.) Here's my camera and two exposed films of irreplaceable pictures that will be my family's heirlooms for centuries, so don't X-ray...HEY! You sent them through the X-ray machine!

"Please step aside. We have to inspect your bag further." It's the shaving cream can. They didn't like it in Stuttgart.

"What's in this box?" (They like my shaving cream.) Well, it says 'House of 1000 Clocks' so that would suggest a clock.

"Open it." (I'll tear off the tape that says 'House of 1000 Clocks' and let you see.) It's a clock, see? Surprised?

"I must pass it through the X-ray again." (It won't change, except that it might get radioactive.) Go ahead.

"Something is in the corner. What are these?" (Obviously, fragmentation hand grenades.) Weights to make the clock run, and to make the cuckoo come out (oops, I'd better go light on the cuckoo part).

"Hans, are these clock parts? They are? Please wrap the box and repack your bag, and go away and never visit my airline again."

Well, we got on the plane, but my tongue was a little sore from biting it.

We lived for two weeks on a military base, and met some reservist patriots who have put their civilian lives on hold and left their families at home. These folks aren't on the "point of the spear," as they say, but they've been called up to help the full-time military function well. These are people like Steve, Bob, Marlene, Dean and Loralee, who work 12-hour days and get phone calls at night and are rewarded with protestors at the gate. We need these people.

God, bless 'em all. That's a prayer. Bless 'em all.

The Retiree—April, 2003—Deutschland

Germany is full of cars. There isn't room for another one. Our visit was short, and our experience was only in the southwest, but I'm sure the entire country is the same. In order to park another car in Germany, you'd have to wait at the border for someone to leave.

Restaurants have completely inadequate parking lots. Maple Lake restaurants have a total parking area about equal to the entire state of Baden-Wuerttemberg. Cars park carefully there. Cars have to be smaller there. Lots of people walk considerable distances to restaurants and they tend to spend a lot of time at restaurants. They're trying to make it to the next meal, to save another walk.

Our son bought his dream car there, to use for the year he will be on duty as a called-up reservist. It isn't exactly his dream car, but it's as close as he could come and not go broke. It's 4 years old and has 100,000 miles on it, but it's in great shape, and it goes 150 mph. That's unnerving, since the speedometer reads in kph and shows 240 when he's got the hammer down. He put the hammer down whenever the speed limit signs went away on the autobahn. When I see 240 on a speedometer, I begin to cry. I cried a lot.

There are slower cars. And faster ones. Fastest seems to be Porsche, followed by Mercedes and BMW. When the speedometer read 220 and our son pulled over into the right lane, it was usually a Porsche that he was letting fly by. When he returned to the left lane, the nameplates he passed said Volvo, Opel, VW, Peugeot, Renault, and one 1978 Chevrolet police car from San Francisco with its number still painted on the roof.

In town, little short cars abound. These cars had tiny engines and names like Seat, Toledo, Smart, Bora, Zafira, Twingo, Fun, Pink Floyd, Demio, and practically anything else you could think of. There are still a few Ducks around but no Trabants; they've all failed emission standards. They park anywhere, sidewalks included, unless they see something like Verboten written on the wall. It doesn't take much of a towtruck to haul away a Smart, so they pay close attention to words like that.

Scattered around the Autobahns are little flash cameras hooked up to radar. Woops, one might say, and in the mail would come a bill for speeding. Once you say "woops," it's too late. You're already in the system and you may as well go transfer some money to your checking account. It's a fascinating system, and one can only hope it doesn't show up on I-94.

Military rules for driving are stringent. To drive on a military reservation, permission must be granted by the Joint Chiefs of Staff or higher. I didn't use my international driving permit. Passengers can hang on with both hands without having to cling to a steering wheel. That's helpful.

Stuttgart has a dandy subway system. We caught the train above ground, and it dove underground after a couple stops. Two of us together could figure out which direction to take the S3 train to and from Vaihingen, no small accomplishment considering the size of the Stuttgart station. When the schedule says the train arrives at 1535, it arrives at 1535 precisely and is but a memory by 1536. We were reassured that we were going the right direction by that German punctuality, so we didn't end up in Bad Somethingorother instead of Stuttgart.

It would be nice to have a subway extend to Maple Lake, but we'd need 100,000 people to ride it in order for it to pay off. And that would mean little parking spots, cobblestones, walking to the restaurant, and maybe driving one of those pocket-sized wind-up toys. After considering that, it's nice to be home.

The Retiree—April, 2003—Repairs

Looks like we're short of toilet paper, but I find out in time. There's another roll on the top shelf across the room, behind the towels. I can reach it, but it slips out of my hand. I grab for it but am off balance and I fall into the stall shower in the corner. To stop my fall, I grab the hot water handle, and the pipe breaks off inside the wall.

The water comes out in force, and runs quickly into our rather unstable crawl space. Saturated by the spring thaw, the wall needs only a little impetus to give way into the half-basement where all my tools and motors are.

Unsupported now, the outside wall caves in, knocking out a gas line and starting a fire from the flame on our overzealous water heater. The blaze soon finds a propane tank and two outboard motors, quickly creating a greater conflagration.

I rush to a safe vantage point near the garage, only to watch dry grass ignite. The neighbor's house is soon engulfed. The blaze continues on to the next house and to a field of dry grass. Pushed by the wind, the fire reaches the airport, touching off the tail of a plane. The pilot leaps out but the plane zooms wildly into the air and crashes into the town's water tower, which falls onto the fire engine, erasing hope for a quick end to the disaster.

Meanwhile, the well continues to pump into the yard, washing a stream to the beached boat, pooling up and finally releasing, washing the dock off the yard and into the lake, where it continues to roll until it disappears into 30 feet of water.

I back the car away from the disaster scene and jump out, only to find that I've left it in gear. It heads for the lake, following the dock into deeper water. Cars can really make good distance when they've got a nice steep hill to give them a start.

Through all the chaos, the phone rings. I reach in through the kitchen window, broken but not yet engulfed in flame. A voice asks me my formal, seldom-used full name and offers me insurance on my credit card.

Then, my wife comes into the room. "Haven't you finished grouting the bathroom tile yet?" she says. "What are you doing there, anyway?"

"Oh, nothing," I respond. "Just taking a break. Just making a few notes for another Retiree column. Maybe the grout is dry. I'll check. Are we out of toilet paper?"

The Retiree—April, 2003—Cleaning

We have a bunch of people coming over for refreshments and talking about lakes and eating and trips and eating and Babylonian empires and eating and current events and eating and Bible study. I'll vacuum, I say, and you can dust and shake rugs and wipe off things.

Dog has a really high interest in vacuum cleaners. Our Hoover has become her herd. She follows it wherever it goes. Most of the vacuuming that takes place is because of her, and she has a need to see everything that takes place.

Why are you carrying that plug out there, says Wife, in more of a command voice than a question. Because the vacuum runs on electricity, I reply insolently, to my dismay. When I do it I plug it in over there, she says. I'll vacuum, I say, you dust and shake rugs and wipe off things. The cord won't reach, I've done this before, she says. I know, I'll plug it there after I'm done here, I say. I used to write procedures and do methods work, I say, again to my dismay, and I can do this with only two replugs. Okay, she says, in a tone that means you'll be sorry but go ahead.

Dog is immediately overwhelmed with a desire to herd the vacuum into the corner of the porch. I tell her politely to get out of the way. She moves fully five inches back. I charge. She moves five feet back. I pluck Chinese ladybug out of corner, move binoculars and flowerpot. Dog returns to take up vigil. I instruct her again, in louder voice.

I devise an elegant method of vacuuming that involves cross patterns. Dog gets in way. I tell her that she should go away in quite certain terms. Wife puts her outside.

Elegant method is revised to include snowplowing motions to clear chairs and end tables. I am quite taken with my brilliance. Wife is less than enchanted. Dog reappears. Wife says she asked to return to her herd. I re-instruct dog on imperatives of cleaning, barely avoiding reference to her (the dog's) ancestry.

Sufficient dog fur to build another dog is collected. Dog appears to want another dog built so she can expand her vacuum shepherd pack. Japanese ladybug is picked out of corner. Taiwanese ladybug is chipped out from under baseboard.

Vacuum won't reach behind toilet, so I use alternative manual hand motion to collect dog fur and Vietnamese ladybug shell. Fur collection will require EPA certificate for disposition. Dog appears behind toilet. I inform her of her error. Wife inquires as to what I am doing. Tee trinken und abwarten, I reply. What, she says. German, I reply. Why can't you complain in Norwegian like all your relatives, she says, in something of an accusatory tone. Das macht nichts, I say, to my immediate regret.

Snowplowing motion doesn't work on bed or dresser. I narrowly avoid breaking vacuum headlight. Dog goes away quickly under torrent of demands. Wife collapses on kitchen floor with wet rag in hand, asking why I didn't get fur under bookcase. Nobody is going to lie on floor to look under bookcase, I say, again regretting it before I finish.

Maybe we don't need to invite a bunch of people over for awhile. Maybe I should insist that we have nothing but outside picnics. Once people are covered in marshmallow and ashes, they don't care if the house is full of fur.

But, then, the dog has to be entertained.

The Retiree—May, 2003—Trip

Taking our charge seriously (Retirees Must Travel) we went on another trip. This one was once again to the Land of the Fogies, Branson, Missouri. For us, it was a visit to friends and relatives who have chosen to live in that area. Naturally, we got a deal on lodging, because that's what seniors do.

A new unit of measure became apparent on our trip. We developed the McD, for McDonald's. About 3 McDs equal an hour of freeway travel. We drove 36 McDs to get to Branson. It was 12 McDs to Kansas friends and relatives. Home again was two legs of 18 and 14 McDs. The closest relatives were only 2 McDs away. One cup of coffee (senior) lasts about one McD but we didn't try to get a free refill on cups bought at another McD. Traveling across the country on 29 cents seemed a little cheap even for seniors. After all, we had those free breakfasts in the motels to stock up on cream and sugar and apples.

Branson may be the only place one can watch a Dutchman play two grand pianos at once with a water show in the background. Forty thousand gallons of water squirt all over the place while mobile pianos scoot magically around the stage barely within reach of the Dutchman. We had our choice of two free shows in our package. The lady said, "Here's your first choice. What else from this list would you like? This one and that one and that one aren't open yet."

Branson seems to be the home of old entertainers. Maybe there are cities where old people from other occupations gather. Maybe Penobscot is the home of old milkmen who stumble around delivering milk that has expired dates. Maybe Fargo holds a bunch of Y2K programmers, writing COBOL-D code to do batch programs. Maybe Yazoo City provides comfort to retired dentists who still pull teeth. Come to think of it, I saw an article about dentists in Romania...

Anyway, we found everyone cordial except for a few people like me and one of my wife's cousins, who'd rather complain. How would you know who was good and happy without having some of us around to provide a contrast?

We were in the midst of record tornadoes. Nothing new for us. We lived through record heat in the South, and watched record snow in New England, and watched record rain flow through our house here. The people in Missouri and environs are good at helping out when disaster strikes. Evidently they have a lot of practice. Every other day was tornado day there.

Many other wonderful events occurred on our trip. We saw a beautiful garden that made my wife jealous, looked at magnificent antiques (including relatives), saw the wonders of medical science in the form of recovering patients, and learned that everyone we talked to has an old car to work on or fondle.

Travel is so enlightening, so broadening. Wife is out in the garden, and I am heading to the garage to chip rust off the old Bronco for a one-McD trip to Buffalo.

The Retiree—May, 2003—Farming

The sad part of Spring has come. I planted radishes and carrots along the edge of the daylily patch, and now they've come up.

So far I haven't had to do much. I bought the seeds, and one day in a frenzy of work and excitement I scratched a row around the patch and dribbled the seeds in. I stuck the packages into the ground with sticks, the way my mother used to do.

Now the new little leaves are above the ground, the radishes in a neat curvy row, and the carrots in a bunch where the last two-inch rain sent them. I trimmed the daylilies back so the new plants could get the requisite sunshine. There they sit in their crowded little neighborhoods.

I know what has to come next. I must thin them out.

How can I deny life to some of those hopeful little plants, just for the survival of their neighbors? Who am I to choose plant 15 over plants 14 and 16 as a survivor? Where would I get that sort of authority? Who appointed me the Angel of Death for those helpless little radishes and carrots?

They all look so willing to grow, so able, so green. Plant 32 is just as likely to give me a nice round radish as is plant 33. Of course I can't tell which plant has a rock under it, or which one will get its top eaten off by some other vile, murderous, evil creature. Maybe if I took plant 32 instead of plant 33, that evil creature would not take notice, and would go away. But then evil creatures have to eat, too, and I certainly don't have the will or authority to deny them their meals. And there are still those rocks.

What I need is a schedule of vermin meals. I need to know when and where the next vole or bunny or cutworm expects to dine. Then my culling process would be less distasteful, as the plants would be used appropriately, although they would be stricken down in the prime of their youth, never to attain maturity, to go to seed, to have little plants that look up to them.

I'll do that. I'll publish a list of vermin meal times, and hope the little buggers read and follow it. I'll have to use something that will be useful to vermin. Maybe a sundial. Maybe I can set out a light on a timer. That should do it. I'll put the selected plants and vermin meal times on a plate under the light, and they will find it. Eventually, by associating the light with the published list, the little creatures will be able to read and follow my list.

There are raccoons around, though. They'd eat the whole bunch of vegetables. They've already dug into my sod to find grubs, more than once. They don't like the light. And squirrels dig up flower bulbs, and probably like carrots too. I don't think they're interested in reading.

I know. I'll camp out on the roof some night with a few bricks, or maybe those rocks that are spoiling my vegetables. Then when the little vandals come for their plunder, I'll smash them flat. That'll teach them. And it'll get rid of the rocks.

Farming isn't easy, is it?

The Retiree—June, 2003—Kids

Part of the routine of having house guests is entertaining them, especially when most of the guests are your grandchildren. When the guests include girls age 4 and 6, the entertainment can include one of those noisy play rooms at a fast food restaurant. It does for us, anyway.

The entertainment for adults at such a place is exclusively made up of eavesdropping on the other adults in attendance. The other adults are usually mothers, of whom about a third are pregnant. They and their charges must of necessity talk in a modified scream in order to be heard. In the resulting cacophony, I think I heard a variety of names that reveal trends in modern society. No Barbaras or Johns nowadays. Here are a few that I think I heard over the crash of little bodies:

Brigand, Arnica, Bragan, Rabies, Gaby (maybe the same as Rabies), Porcelain, Chase (Manhattan?), Polycolor, and Seville.

Now, I admit to some inattention, since our own charges were usually yelling in my ears, but I do think modern parents have gone a little over the edge with the privilege of naming their progeny. These children seem to be normal rural and suburban children, but harnessing them with names such as the above would seem to lead them into a life of crime or to become recluses. Maybe we're better for that. Some of them needed locking up right now.

Our own grandchildren have trendy modern names, too, but they can at least be recognized as human names. In fact, the youngest has perhaps the oldest name, but he seems to be content with it, and it will be easy for him to spell. I won't list the names of our grandchildren, since they are too young to give me legal permission, and they could very well sue me. At least that's what I would do in a similar situation.

A bunch of shirt-tail Swede relatives from Dassel invited us over the other day to get acquainted. These were second cousins whom I'd never met. The cousins were trying to make some attachment to their past; something our grandparents had neglected and our parents had ignored. Gas rationing, distance, and maybe pure dislike, who knows, had kept us apart. Swedes used trendy names back in the old days, but the trends were different. Their family tree includes such classics as Boel, Gustava, Ingeborg, Karna, Nels, Otiliana, Matte, and Peter (?), as well as a bunch of names with umlauts that can't be pronounced with an American tongue.

On my Norwegian side, names were sensible, at least to Norwegians. The girls had names like Ingrun, Kari, Oddveig, Milda, and the ever-popular Ingeborg. All the boys were named John, for maybe six generations, saving on monogrammed hand-me-downs.

I suppose there'll be a batch of bored space-age relatives a hundred years from now looking over old digital pictures and wondering at those old-fashioned names. "Look at this one," they'll say. "Jerry. How'd he ever tolerate that? And here's a Barbara. What were they thinking? Honestly, Jolt, if Erk and Smosh ever hear about that, they'll split a gossan."

The Retiree—July, 2003—Frog

I found a dead frog in a mousetrap in my basement. To me, that means it's been raining too hard. Now, I don't mind a little moisture for the plants, even though my radishes and carrots have been overwhelmed by day-lilies. But when a frog gets caught in a mousetrap, I get a little frustrated. It's too much.

The frog looked familiar, although they all look pretty much alike to me. Last fall I followed a frog in through the overhead door when I was putting some summer stuff away. The rascal headed for the workbench. I tried to persuade him to go out and dig into the mud like all his buddies were doing, but he ducked the kick and went under the furnace. Fully expecting frog jerky by spring, and not wanting to crawl around on the floor, I forgot about him.

He could have been free, roaming the lakefront and doing frog things, but instead he elected to become like us humans, living in a house and eating basement spiders (although I seldom eat bugs), taking an occasional nap instead of hibernating. And his conversion to human surroundings would have worked, too, if it hadn't been for that miserable six-inch rain and the usual reappearance of a puddle around the floor drain, which isn't really a drain at all, but a stone sump. Obviously he stumbled upon the trap, and tiring of his all-meat diet, decided to make a cheese sandwich. Whack.

There's a lesson for us in that frog's unfortunate demise, but I'm danged if I can figure out what it is.

Only a short time before the frog episode, our loaner-dog (on loan from our Caribbean daughter) found a toad near the driveway. Being a herding dog, she tried to herd the toad into the garage or some other civilized location so she could conduct experiments on amphibian life. Maybe I give her too much credit, but they are supposed to be smart dogs.

The toad objected to being herded in typical toadian fashion. Dog grabbed toad, and toad turned sour or something. I'm not about to try licking toads, but the dog found out that they taste extremely bad, and she spent some considerable time spitting on the driveway. I thought she was going to croak. The toad did, audibly, but with its defenses mounted was able to escape into the flowers, where presumably it is still licking its wounds with that wretched-tasting tongue. We don't think the dog learned anything. She still tries to herd Labradors and the Schwan's man even though she's been discouraged multiple times from doing so. There's a lesson in that episode, too, but again it's beyond me.

Maybe the lesson is that bad things happen to good animals as well as people, because we're all basically rotten. I suppose that's it. I know I am.

The Retiree—July, 2003—Liberty

When I decided to end my third retirement and re-enter the work force, it soon became apparent that I'd made a big mistake. The opportunity I took was in Hartford, the very heart of the Yankee stronghold. I moved there after I'd become sensitized to the world of the Rebel, as an adopted child of the Confederacy, warmed by the Carolina sun and softened by the attitudes of the genteel South.

I couldn't even (and still can't) pronounce Atheneum or Faneuil Hall, and I have a lot of trouble with Italian restaurant menus, all of which are definite clues to the probability of a difficult adjustment. Gentility and sensitivity are rare commodities in New England. I don't think I ever found any, and brought precious little along with me.

I did come out of that experience into my fourth retirement with a better understanding of the unpleasantness that we here call the Civil War (although from what I've read, it was very uncivil) and in the Old South we called the War of Northern Aggression.

All this was brought back to mind by the passing of Strom Thurmond, whose name pops up in a great number of public places in Columbia and all over South Carolina. We once went to a Peach Festival in a small South Carolina town back around 1993 and there was Strom at a young 90 years, astride a horse, of all things. How they got him up there was unexplained, but he did stay up there for the whole parade. We were all very impressed.

Friends from the Old South recently sent us a really elaborate e-mail notice regarding The Sixteenth Annual Carolina Celebration of Liberty. It's in color (red, white, and blue) and includes dramatic patriotic music. When we lived in Columbia the celebration was held on the State Capitol steps, with choir and band music, flags, buntings, politicians, and military units. One year it rained, and everyone moved 4 or 5 blocks to the First Baptist Church, the biggest church in town. The crowd overflowed onto the street. Our friends found a few seats open in the very front, a row behind generals, the governor, representatives, clergy, and Strom Thurmond, where the genteel Southerners would dare not go. We were quite impressed by our exalted companions, and even listened to some of the speakers.

This year the Celebration of Liberty was dedicated to the return of troops from Iraq, and drew about 20,000 people to "The USC" (they had the name first) football stadium. On July Fourth each year, another classic impressive elaborate spectacular grand awe-inspiring stirring stunning breathtaking ceremony is held at Columbia's Fort Jackson, where 9,000 troops come marching over the hill to help a huge crowd watch spectacular fireworks. Those Rebels really know how to be patriotic. We miss that.

Minnesota celebrations aren't quite the same as those Carolina extravaganzas. Somehow, watching fireworks over Pleasant Lake is a little low-key. Four overweight veterans carrying war surplus M-1's instead of 9,000 marching troops may seem paltry or minimalist. Maybe it's because of my own low-key Scandinavian heritage, but somehow I still like that.

The Retiree—August, 2003—Trip

As required (we are retired), we went on another trip. Branson was the cheapest place we could go, as a brother-in-law wanted company at his timeshare.

Fifty-nine steps took us to the door. Fifty-five down and four up. We brought our luggage down 55 up 4, and then went down 4 up 55 to get the food, and down 55 up 4 and down 4 up 55 to get the camera and down 55 up 4 to collapse.

We went swimming, down 4 and up 55, up the hill, and up another 19. We went back down 19, down 55, up 4 to change, and then down 4 and up 55 to go visit another brother-in-law. They live up only 5 from where we parked the car. Then down 5, drive, down 55, up 4 to collapse again.

Cicadas and tree frogs live there. They start singing at 9:30 after dark in chorus, and they sing until 3:45 in the morning, when they see the paper carrier's truck up the hill. Single-pane glass has no sound-deadening effect. In fact, it collects and magnifies sound.

The place was not bad, overall. Set on a mountainside (mountain by Ozark standards), it had a view of trees. Inside, it was very nice, but of course we spent little time inside. Outside, it needed a few little things, like new walls and new sidewalks and a new deck. The roof was new, but done by someone in a hurry, evidently. Fortunately the brother-in-law had traded from his normal digs to get a week in the Ozarks and didn't have to worry about new siding.

Branson is still full of septuagenarians and octogeraniums with canes and walkers. With any luck at all we will join that crowd so nothing bad will be said about them. However, the entertainers will find smaller crowds as that World War II audience becomes less mobile. Some of them have trouble standing to salute the flag and receive the applause of grateful citizens at the various performances now. Come to think of it, the entertainers will also find themselves restricted to walkers and wheelchairs as well, so maybe everything will work out.

One does tend to wonder what will happen to those theaters, though, after age descends on performers and audience alike. An appeal will have to go out to a younger crowd. Even now, some younger people are observed at things like Dolly Parton's Dixie Stampede. All those performers are young and agile. Even the ringmaster walked out unaided. And no one could eat all that food without being just a little young at heart.

I suppose there are grander things to worry about, such as world peace and the ecology. But if I don't worry about the fate of those grand theaters, who will? And how will the Ozarks look once the lights are turned out? And where will Dolly retire? And what happens to all those horses when there are no more shows? And who'll buy all those American flags?

Most of all, who is going to go down 55 steps and up 4 and back down 4 and up 55 with a walker? It makes my head hurt to think about it. I think I'll go take an aspirin, or maybe some Geritol.

The Retiree—August, 2003—Marriage

"How about a pack of those plastic bullet-hole stickers and a bottle of mustard-based barbecue sauce?" As soon as I say things like that, I regret it. Those comments can only lead to further discussion, and it isn't always amicable. The question from my wife was, "What do you think would be a good wedding present for that daughter of your hunting buddy?"

Women shouldn't ask questions like that. Men don't have a clue what sort of things are suitable for presents. I wouldn't think of suggesting a crystal bud vase, even though we seem to end up with one of those for every wedding.

Lots of questions aren't fit for men to answer. Such things as "don't you think my hair is awful" or "have I gained weight" cannot be answered in any way without getting into trouble. Not answering those questions also gets one into trouble. I haven't found a way to answer or avoid answering, but then we've only been married 40 years.

Another question to cause certain discussion is "what are you looking at" when you are driving past a female bicyclist. You have to look, after all, so you don't run over her, but you aren't expected to look at critical parts of her anatomy, and that includes looking in the rear-view mirror after passing her, no matter what kind of halter top she's wearing.

So far, our marriage has overcome all the hurdles I've thrown up in front of it. That's a tribute to the woman I chose. Actually, I don't remember choosing her, as though I had a stable of beauties waiting to be picked. It just happened, I guess, while I was trying to figure out what the rest of my life should look like, and now I can't imagine any other way for my life to look. But I don't want to get sentimental here. It could ruin those conversations we have when I'm supposed to pick out presents or match colors.

Maybe I'm the only husband who doesn't remember what his wife is wearing when we go somewhere, but I don't think so. It's easy to remember what she looks like after 40 years, but there are lots of silver-haired, svelte beauties out there (that should help for awhile) who look alike from the back. If I couldn't remember whether she was wearing a blue denim jacket or that nice patterned dress she wore Sunday, she'd be hard to pick out from across the stadium or field or store. I'd be hard pressed to describe her to the police if she finally decides to leave me because I was watching some white shorts go through the produce aisle.

One redeeming factor exists for my peace of mind. Just about every man has the same problems that I do. My wife knows that. All wives know that. Leaving me and finding another one would only compound the problem. She'd not only have the generic male tendencies to handle, she'd have to learn a whole new set of individual quirks that we all have, admit it, as individuals.

That's where I stand regarding husband-wife relationships today. I probably won't change. Remember, don't look for me for advice. This isn't an advice column.

So far, nobody's taken my advice anyway.

The Retiree—July, 2003—Eats

Retirees can't just coast along. We have duties to perform. One of ours is to see that my 92-year-old stepmother gets fed and has her bills paid on Sundays. She takes us to lunch to compensate us for our efforts. She tells us that she pays someone else for getting her drugs and groceries, so we take her out to eat and she pays.

It's no trouble, except for figuring out where she really wants to go. If we suggest chicken, she's had that for the last three days. If we suggest Italian, she went there yesterday. She'll say, "You pick a place but I'd really like a good hamburger and maybe a glass of wine or a boilermaker or a couple snorts of redeye," and we decide that we didn't want chicken after all.

While waiting for service the other day we observed that eating out has changed from the old days. You may have noticed some of these changes.

Baseball caps are important at some restaurants. Rules for wearing the cap follow rules of the University of Minnesota Band. That is, they wore their hats frontwards if the team lost, and backwards if the team won. Baseball caps are thusly worn frontwards if the meal is bad and backwards if it is good. Anyone can wear a baseball cap while eating, and teen boys must do so. My Mom would have been furious. So would Stepmom, if she could see a little better.

Eating with an open mouth has become fashionable. Most teens do that. Stuff falls out while they are talking, which they do incessantly. They also may eat while sitting cross-legged in a booth. It hurts for retirees to sit that way. I tried.

Widowers can be identified by their clothing. They wear teal-blue pants and Guyabarra shirts—you know, those lace-trimmed ones with four pockets—or polyester outfits with string ties. Widows dress in their finest and order quietly, observing the widowers, looking for one with matching clothes and a tucked-in shirttail.

We were almost forced to observe one couple because of the husband's behavior. He was competing for the Chronic Complainer of the Year Award, and stood head and shoulders above his competition. On the way in, he announced that he wanted copious amounts of food and would make lots of noise if he didn't get it. He sat hunkered over his plate, griping while sorting through his hash, bellowing for more iced tea. He berated his wife for everything, and she would have left him in an instant if she'd been a little less ugly. He said he'd pay because she didn't have any money, and when she said she had some, he berated her again for not telling him.

Across the room were two women, maybe mother and daughter. There was no conversation between them. Both of them read books for the entire time we were there. We suspect that they had no knowledge of what they ate.

Now that I look back, I complain, too. There are times when I'd like to stand up and say, "You there! Shut up or get out! Smile! Sit up straight! Stop combing your hair! Close your mouth! Get your elbows off the table! Put away the book! Tuck in that shirt! Say please and thank you! Eat your carrots!" Some day I'll do that. You can visit me in jail.

The Retiree—August, 2003—Play

"Play while it is day, before the night comes when no man can play." That's Biblical and I've always tried to follow that injunction.

WOOPS. I just looked it up, and it says, "WORK while it is day, before the night comes…"

Well, I guess I blew that one. It's too late for me to go back to work. I just have to live with the consequences now that I've established my inappropriate habits. I don't have much recourse. I just have to keep on playing. It's that old-dog-new-tricks thing again; the last rationalization of old people who don't want to change.

Back when my boss thought I was working in systems, I ran across lots of people who had no intention of changing. It's not just a trait of old people. It seems to be a characteristic common to everyone. Things become habit. I always brush my teeth using my right hand. I always mow the yard from the top down to the lake. I always kick the dog with my right foot. I always mouse with my left hand, and I KNOW that's the way we should all do it, so we can write down error messages with the right hand before the screen goes blank. I always put the anchor down on the right side of the pontoon boat. And I am NOT going to change.

In systems work, the trick was to make the victim, or client, think the change being proposed was his or her idea, and then the change would take place. It didn't matter if I didn't get the credit. The important thing was to get the change done.

One problem with not getting the credit was that it appeared that I didn't do anything. Maybe that explains my five retirements. That, and my misunderstanding of the Biblical exhortation above.

Regardless, I plan to keep on playing. Next come two more trips. One's a bargain trip to Las Vegas, and the other's a trip to the Caribbean, where we old parents can leech off our daughter. You may wonder how we can make so many trips on a limited, fixed income. The answer is credit cards and equity loans. Irresponsible, yes, but it's the American way.

Playing isn't always easy. Companies find out that you like to play, and then they call with new and intriguing ways to charge you for playing. And since between retirements one and two, I did a lot of phone calling, I am a little sensitive to the feelings of that caller on the other end of the line. I don't sign up for those government-sponsored lists of people who don't want to be called, just so I don't have to hurt anyone's feelings—until they call, that is. If they sound like they're reading a script, I try to get them off track. If they sound like they are an old friend, Jerry buddy, I try to make them feel like a jerk. If they have something that sounds really good, I tell them to send me a letter. I don't buy. Some day they'll understand that, maybe. Meanwhile, I get all those calls the rest of you used to get before you signed up on a government list.

That's my approach to playing. It's an amalgam of misunderstanding, ignorance and irrationality. I learned it from my relatives, and added some stubborn quirks of my own. You may use any of my approaches free of charge. I won't care. I'll be off somewhere, playing.

The Retiree—July, 2003—Eats

French dinner. Sounded good to us, as we were recovering from another of those onslaughts of relatives that seem to occur with some frequency on the lake. There were three couples in attendance, a good number for dinner; small enough to hear what's being said, and big enough to allow time to think up smart remarks.

Your typical French restaurant isn't located on a Minnesota lake, but Minnesotans do what they have to do in order to expand their cultural horizons. Our collective horizons weren't exactly expanded, although we learned some about the rich buggers who built on this or that lake over the past year. We also learned that our waiter could squeeze his entire body through a 7" space. The waiter said getting his ears through was the hardest part. He didn't demonstrate his skill, although he did crawl under our table to level a leg, and that took a certain degree of dexterity.

Again, here are a few random remarks from the dinner. Some are baldfaced lies, to protect the innocent and provide cover for the guilty.

"What's this thing on the menu? It's the same in English as in French. Beans? Why don't they just say beans, then? No wonder they lose all those wars. They can't understand the orders. Waiter, are you French? You look like a Swede to me."

"Sicker than a dog. They found a heart problem and a couple tumors. Should live for a while yet, but it doesn't look good. I think she's 88, maybe 90. Just came back from a trip to California. Drove herself. Alone. Planning to go to Michigan. But she's sick, believe me."

"We stayed for a month in Brownsville. Lots of Mexicans, lots of Minnesotans. We don't speak Spanish and have a little trouble with Texan. Used sign language a lot—you know, pointing at tamales and grapefruit, that kind of thing."

"The bathroom in the camper is sort of limited. The tank holds for about 3 days before a dump. You say you have that problem from time to time, too?"

"There was a little water problem. It wasn't disclosed at the sale, so there could be a lawsuit. Something about a river running through the basement. Good fishing, though, especially around the water heater. Some people do nothing but complain."

"Four thousand a foot for lakefront around Brainerd. The tax man is crazy with glee. Everyone else is bonkers, too. One guy tore down a $350,000 house to put up a little nicer place. Some people need things like indoor pools, saunas, grand staircases. ballrooms, libraries..."

"There's a house available next to Glensheen. That would be nice, except in the winter, which is October through May. It rained like a cow...you know...all the time we were there, and it was about 50 degrees. Pretty nice day, for Duluth."

"Then the Devil says, 'Those, in that pile over there? They're Minnesotans. They're too wet and cold to burn.'"

"Come and see the camper." On the way home we did. It was lovely. As the mosquitos carried Carol across the yard, we said "Au reservoir." Recapturing Carol, we ended a pleasant evening, still wondering why the French don't just say "beans."

The Retiree—September, 2003—
Technology

I needed some 2x6's to create something almost useful, and it was raining. I didn't want to get wet. So, in order to avoid starting a different project, I resorted to reading my computer magazine.

Advances in personal computing in the past couple years have put me at an enormous disadavantage to those who keep current. It's hard to believe that any but the most dedicated hackers can keep up with technology. I can scarcely read the magazine any more. Anyway, I never was much for that high-tech stuff. Naturally, a few questions and comments came to mind from my reading. I really made the right decision when I went the user route instead of the technical path back a dozen years ago before my fourth retirement. Maybe you will have answers to the following, although secretly I hope you are as out of touch as I am.

Does Microsoft have a back door in their Windows OS? Is that what Gates was trying to avoid? Gates, doors, windows? What is going on, anyway?

Are the LoveSan virus, worms, Autorooter, Mozilla, Red Hat, and maybe the GNU public license going to make ActiveX redesign necessary?

Is Midrange Screenblast enough, or would Adobe Premiere Pro be worth the cost? Maybe hyper-threading tests would make Pinnacle a contender. Looks like Ulead Cool with Muvee or Imaginate would help, too, if you don't decide on Smartsound or Vegas. Maybe it would be better if you have steganography or a secure USB drive.

I don't have a NetNanny Chat Monitor or a Peachtree accounting system. RIM BlackBerry (these people love to put capital letters in the middle of words) and Portege (with a couple accent marks on the e's) seem to indicate that I shouldn't get a PDA for awhile, until I can figure out just why I need one. Maybe I can get some information from Blogdigger, Daypop, Feedster, Fyuze, or another of the finding feeds.

Do I need a wireless net or will a hacker exploit it with rogue MIDI files and migrant Mafia to make a zombie? Maybe a PestPatrol Port Checker would reduce malicious code or buffer overflow. I need a white paper on SonicWALL to check on phantom administrators.

Well, you get the idea. Little by little, I've been made a dinosaur. If I decided to go for re-employment, I don't think I'd make it in the computer world. Some big shot would come by my desk and ask me to reeve the bluton before the next tolcom turned defong, and I'd have to sit there like a ninny and await my certain expulsion into retirement number six.

I'm going to get me some 2x6s. There are some steel wheels in the crawl space that I can use. I'll build a flat truck to haul in the dock. Nobody will ask me if the drive is secure, I won't need any passwords, and the only worms I'll have to worry about are under the deck, where I think I left the hammer.

The Retiree—September, 2003—Reunion

I went to my high school class reunion in the Big City the other night. What a revelation that was. Those people are getting OLD. I wonder what they were thinking when they saw me?

Some smart-aleck put our class pictures on key rings, so we could see ourselves in our original hair. Why did our mothers ever let us out of the house when we combed our hair that way? I let our kids get away with the same thing, the absurdities that the young foist upon themselves. If all parents did the appropriate amount of complaining to stop that, though, kids would likely be wearing powdered wigs or coonskin caps. Come to think of it, that wouldn't have been so bad. Then we'd still look like the kids, which I quickly found out we don't. But our kids don't look like they did when they graduated, either.

I sat next to the premiere cheerleader in our entire class of a couple hundred. I don't think I would ever have dared to do that in high school. Turns out she's still good looking and more or less slender, but I don't think she can do the splits any more. She's younger than I, having started kindergarten at four and a half. Boy, did that half year make a difference. She married a classmate, and he looked younger than just about anyone else there.

My class had three or four convicted felons. Only one of them attended, same as last time, but this time it was a different felon. That's not too bad a record, out of 200 or so. They seem to have grown out of their lawbreaking tendencies and after doing the appropriate time are evidently contributing to society as fine upstanding taxpayers who don't even drink too much any more. It's gratifying to see that. Three others in the class reported on a couple nights spent in jail in Rockford, Illinois, back around 1952, but that wasn't for a felony. It took them over 50 years to admit it.

Some 38 classmates are no longer living. That's about 19%, a reasonable number considering the passage of 50 years, as long as I wasn't one of them. Our class avoided some hazards by graduating between wars. Hardly anybody got shot, maybe none in military action.

Six people couldn't be found. Maybe they're in the slammer. We think they're alive. They just didn't like the rest of us very much. I've felt like that from time to time, too.

We couldn't afford fast cars. That saved a few lives. Our idea of a fast car was Jere's '48 Plymouth convert, or Paul's dad's bathtub Nash. Dean went 45 on Minneapolis' Fremont Avenue in low gear once or twice in his dad's '52 Plymouth, and we think some of the football players found ways to break laws on highway 55 by Lake Sarah, but they haven't admitted anything yet. Marv drove his dad's '48 Studebaker a little wildly on his way to cross-country meets but since his license required him to use a seat cushion so he could see out the windshield, he didn't try anything really risky. And our other Marv (we had two) couldn't use or didn't like to use second gear in his dad's '39 Buick so he was no risk either. Now the cars of choice are vans to carry grandchildren around.

There were a few for whom the 50th was their first reunion. Since they had a good time, they may show up for the 75th or maybe the 100th. We always had a few slow starters in our class.

We ate too much, stayed up too late, talked too much, and laughed a lot. It was great. I sure hope we all last until the 55th reunion, if we have one.

I'd really like to go to the next one in five years. But not a moment sooner.

The Retiree—September, 2003—Dips

Fifty-one degrees and there they went, into the lake. "The water feels warm, once you get used to it," they said, but nobody believed it. Our usually-sensible world-traveler son, back from his active duty in Europe, had dropped his fishing rod overboard and didn't want to go home without it.

Some of us tend toward less radical solutions to water-related disasters. Indeed, we tried a variety of remedies to recover the rod. We had already looked overboard from the pontoon boat and made soft clucking noises, shaking our heads, commiserating, extending condolences. Then we took out the rowboat with a few helpers—the permanent magnet-on-a rope, some heavy spoons on 30-pound line, oars, the roof rake. The magnet refused to find brass or graphite, the roof rake insisted on bringing up gobs of weeds, the spoons wouldn't descend to the bottom. So, sensibly, we gave up. After all, his sister's rod has been at the bottom of the lake for the past 20 years or so, and it seemed suitable for his to join it. No use getting all upset over a lost cause.

There I was, putting away nylon cord and spoons and the roof rake, when down he came from the house in my swimming suit, soon followed by his cousin in cutoffs, both threatening to find the rod and reel regardless of the consequences.

I've seen that determination in our son before, usually in regard to things over which I have no control. Once he decided to jog a dozen miles or so in a sort of contrition for breaking a window. Another time he determined to fix a steering column on his car, and spent an entire weekend unwinding incomprehensible wires and making it work. He usually came out well, although a little the worse for wear. When he was a kid, we could threaten him or tie him to a chair, but since college and marriage and the service he's been someone else's concern for the most part. His wife has the job now. We can watch.

So we watched as he dove off the dock and grappled with our weed patch. Not to be outdone, his cousin had to wade in, too. And another generation, the kindergartener son of the cousin, started stripping right there on the dock. His mom, already familiar with the determination of the two flounderers, said go ahead, we drive by a number of hospitals to get home.

Of course the quest was impossible, and of course they found the thing. The cousin found a lure hanging on his thigh, and at the other end, a graphite rod and stainless reel. They emerged, the three of them, festooned with weeds and smiling, after swimming a victory lap around the dock. They insisted they weren't cold, and that we should all get invigorated similarly, to which we responded, "You're bonkers, all three of you."

The living room has cooled off now. Our gas fireplace heated up the room to over 80 and still we couldn't pry the three away from it. The rest of us were prepared to evacuate and let them cook when they finally came to life and got dressed, all the while insisting that it was a good experience and we should all do things like that once in awhile.

Sure, we said. We'll go into the lake. Just not right now. Maybe later. Like, say, July.

The Retiree—October, 2003—Beetles

There's no doubt that you had an invasion of those Asian lady beetles, just as we did. I spent days sweeping up little spotted orange shells and there seemed to be no end in sight. Checking with relatives in both northern and southern Minnesota, I found that the infestation was the same throughout the whole state. Exactly the same.

Using my lot as a standard, there are about 152,864,640 lots in Minnesota. I got that by multiplying my 1/3 acre or so by Minnesota's 50,954,880 acres. Oh, I know there are roads and waters out there, but those bugs are on the roads and over the waters, too, so I multiplied that fifty million number by 3 to get my number.

I haven't counted exactly, but I must have had about 2,000 little spotted orange bugs piling up by my doorways and windows, and especially in the garage. One's in my defroster. I saw her go there. Excluding her, if everyone had 2,000 bugs, and I'm sure they did, that means there were 305,729,279,999 little spotted orange beetles in Minnesota this year. I'm not counting the one in the defroster because we plan to leave her (lady bug) in Nebraska or Oklahoma or someplace on our next trip.

Our dog eats flies, but she refuses to eat beetles of any kind. We could have saved $24 on dog food if she'd only eat the things. Someone told me the beetles eat mosquitos, but I don't think they do anything useful. All they do is die in the doorway. And they're good at that.

Shells should be good for something. Maybe they could be a substitute for plastic. We had some very durable boxelder bug shells in a wall for many years when the place was a cabin, and these spotted orange shells seem to be at least as durable. Over 300 billion shells, or 600 billion half-shells, would make one heck of a blanket if you could stitch them together. Or if they could be flattened out and glued, you could make—let's see—say 16 to the square inch, that would be 19,108,080,000 square inches of beetle sheeting, if I brought the one in the defroster back. That's 132,695,000 square feet, enough to cover 207,336 houses with lovely spotted orange siding. And I haven't even considered using the legs. There must be 1,834,375,680,000 legs on the little buggers, including the Oklahoma one, and who knows how many little ankle and knee joints. The mind boggles. Almost two trillion legs, four, maybe six or eight trillion little joints. And wings. Wings galore. My calculator can't handle all those wings.

What a wasteful society we are. Think of the businesses we could open up. Farms with silos full of beetle shells, markets with old ladies making shell weavings, traders in beetle futures, huge factories gluing shells together, stamping machines making beetle siding—the future belongs to those with imagination, those who think "out of the box," those with vision, those who can figure out how to sweep the little pests off a cement floor.

Well, I'm retired, or I'd be in the forefront of those shakers and movers who see an opportunity and run with it. Maybe you can be a leader. Maybe you will be the one we can call "King of the Beetles." If you are, come on over. I've got 2,000 beetles you can have.

The Retiree—October, 2003—Hunting

Hunting season has always been my favorite time. Not that I ever get anything, but there's something special about getting whacked in the eye by corn stalks, getting sand burrs on your socks, getting wet to the knees, having a windburned face and frostbitten fingers all at once. Who wouldn't love it?

Last time out, I hunted with my son and two of his buddies. I have a hunting hat that is older than any one of them.

As a retiree, new and different rules must be applied in order to survive what is becoming a seriously stressful experience. I can't leap tall buildings in a single bound any more—or even a double-strand barbed wire fence. Walking through waist-high swamp grass, while great fun, isn't exactly inspiring any more. Knowing that there are others with the same needs as I, here are some basic rules for looking better than you actually are:

1—Stop frequently. Tell the group you are marking your territory. Bladders weren't made for all-day use any more. If necessary, drop something, such as your glasses, and make a big show of looking for them. Bending over will aid you in catching your breath.

2—Bring something to eat. If you return to the car/truck/van/SUV, make sure you open up whatever it is. The chewier it is, the better. A beef jerky sandwich on a hard roll would be excellent. Nobody could eat such a thing in less than half an hour, and you will be quite rested at the end of the sandwich.

3—Bring plenty of water. Don't use yours, though. Try to use someone else's. If they run short, they will slow down. This applies to the dog as well; it may be distasteful at first, but you can learn to drink out of an ice cream bucket.

4—Whenever possible, offer to post. Other people can drive whatever exists out there toward you. (Luckily, we usually hunt where there are no other creatures.) If something should chance to fly up or run out, shout "Hen!" at the top of your voice, in case you should miss.

5—Follow infantry rules: Lie down whenever possible; sit if you can't lie down; stand when it is impossible to sit; walk only when you have to. Run has left my vocabulary.

6—Hopefully it will rain. It always rains when I hunt, unless it snows. If it should rain, do not be the first to suggest quitting. In fact, ridicule that first person. Tell stories about the lightning storms you hunted through, the times you had to swim back to the truck, the bridges you had to build to get back to civilization. They won't know. They're too young. But take advantage of the first offer to sit out the storm. Be first in the truck. Open a jerky sandwich.

7—Look for advantages. Look for the corn rows where the planter failed, so you'll have twice the space to stagger. Look for deer trails, beaver trails, ATV trails, and don't tell anyone else when you find one. Take the inside route around anything. Never climb a fence; look for an opening. Remember, you could fall asleep if you try crawling under something.

By now you understand. A little thought can go a long way to preserve the impression of conditioning. Don't save any tricks for next time. Use every advantage. The life you save could be your own. Old and wily always wins over young and enthusiastic.

The Retiree—December, 2003—Flying

Palpable gloom permeated the dank chamber. Silent, somber creatures crouched sullenly around the darkness, some staring lifelessly, some with closed eyes, some glowering menacingly at each other. From time to time a groan could be heard, accompanied by heavy breathing, gutteral noises, apparent attempts at communication although nothing perceptible, no real activity, took place.

From time to time, an opening in the cavern appeared, from which dull roars and acrid smells emanated. Some of the creatures would raise their miserable heads and look hopefully at the opening, only to see it close again. They would return to their torpor, to their miserable existence, moaning, grunting, settling back into the gloom.

At the head of the chamber stood another creature. Although more brightly colored, it exhibited the same torpor, the same gloom, the same look of utter despair. It busied itself at nothing in particular, moving languidly to and fro, ignoring the crouching horde before it. When the chamber entrance opened, it would look up, sometimes moving to the light and smell, always returning to its post, maintaining its look of aloof disdain.

On occasion, one of the creatures would rouse itself and move away to the farther regions of the chamber, sometimes dragging an object behind it. The creature would slowly return after a time, again dragging its possessions behind it, settling again into the dank misery from which it had gone on its apparently fruitless quest.

Then, near the darkest, dankest part of the chamber, one of the creatures slowly rose. Dragging its possessions, it moved between the other creatures, bumping, snarling, growling as it approached the brighter creature. The other creatures watched curiously. Snarling and growling subsided as their attention was drawn to this activity.

The creature raised its head, looked directly at the brighter creature, and attempted communicating with it. It said, with as much conviction as it could muster, "Just when is flight 2096 going to board, anyway? I've got a connection in Chicago to make!"

The Retiree—December, 2003—
Correspondence

Gloria N. Excelsis stopped over the other day. She used to work with me at the Big Insurance Company, located downtown in the Big City. We were complete opposites in temperament, politics, management styles, dress, religion, and practically every other aspect of life. Naturally, we have kept in touch over the years.

We also got a card from O. Ole Knight and his wife, formerly from their life of splendor among the rich in suburban Connecticut. They had a place in New Hampshire where they could get away from the frustrations of the busy world. They lately retired to Michigan, and while moving lost most of their worldly possessions in a traffic accident after getting rid of the New Hampshire digs. They now live in poverty in a Michigan farming village.

Out West, we get missives from California friends and relatives. One couple is now exiled to Idaho, where he has periodic heart problems and broken limbs, and Yuletide Carol, his wife, has found religion, not yet involving a Shaman. We also fire off notes from time to time to a tennis-playing cousin who'd rather not talk about things such as family.

In the Midwest, we hear regularly from Tom Atumtum, a heart patient and her husband who fell off a ladder and crunched his shoulder into his pelvis. They continue to fake some kind of employment and call it semi-retirement. We also keep in touch with an insurance examiner on the vast American prairie, who travels so much that he no longer remembers where he left his wife. Of course, we visit my sister and her ailing husband on the Leech Lake reservation, only after they have put the bales around their wigwam.

Southerners we still keep up with send us remembrances of the Old South such as fatback, pickled pigs' feet, okra, and various nuts, not the various nuts with which we correspond. We retaliate with wild rice, corncob syrup, pickled hammer-handle-northerns, and the like. Another cousin sends us cards annually but hasn't been seen for years by anyone else in the family. We understand.

Abroad, we have Gunnar Notallowed and other Swedish cousins with whom to be concerned. To date our correspondence has been minimal, since they exhibited a tendency to travel, and we don't want a houseful of foreigners babbling in an alien tongue about our lack of hospitality.

Offshore, we send sewing needles, spare machine parts, computer games, dolls, parking brake cables, and check stubs to help the Caribbean economy surrounding St. Lucia. Augustina there has a variety of requests to enable her to fend off starvation. Not much gets imported to St. Lucia that we don't see first.

Those various nuts are all wonderful people. It takes many years for people to develop major idiosyncracies, and they don't get in touch with us until the idiosyncracies are fully developed. Christmas is the best time to get together, as one tends to have a more forgiving, more placid state of mind during holidays. We love them all. At least, at holiday time.

Come to think of it, maybe that's why we hear from them now. They probably consider us to be their idiosyncratic friends in the Frozen North. Maybe we've misread them all these years. Maybe we are the butt of their jokes, from California to the Caribbean to Sweden.

Oh, well, it cuts both ways. That's what friends are for. Entertainment.

The Retiree—January, 2004—Advice

Retirement requires some training, I have found. There may be classes or lessons on retirement somewhere, but I am too cheap to find one. Come to think of it, that's one of the lessons: How to be cheap so you can subsist on a reduced income. Since I am well into my fifth retirement, I probably have a better background to teach the fundamentals of retirement than most people. Here are a few tips, to whet the appetite and make you want more. If I ever teach a seminar, you'll pay, let's see, $120 for half a day of suggestions. I'm developing my syllabus below.

Travel: Do it now, before you get sick. Something's bound to pop or tear or fester sooner or later, and you don't want to travel with wounds. You should always be planning a trip, and you should never ignore someone who wants to talk about a trip. They might share the cost.

Cars: Buy one that will hold walkers, canes, wheelchairs, and fat butts. Your friends are all getting old, too.

Medicine: Take lots of pills. Doing so will make your doctor and druggist happy, and the more happy healthcare people you can develop, the better. Take a nurse to lunch. A cheap lunch, maybe in a grocery store. One with a drug counter.

Diet: Naturally, those healthcare people will try to improve your diet. I found a doctor who told me chocolate, beer, red wine, and almonds are good for me. Look around for such a doctor, and don't take the advice of anyone who looks at all like a vegetarian.

Eating out: Find early-bird specials. Take home doggie bags, even if they are someone else's. Take the rolls and butter. Put jelly and sugar packets in your pocket. Eat the mints and take toothpicks. Go to funerals—anyone's—and eat afterwards. Same with weddings. Remember, whatever you save can be spent on more pills.

Clothing: Robe and slippers before noon. No doubleknits. Expect to look like a dork, but try not to look like a '70s dork. Review the following point, if you think you can still pull it off.

Attitude: Cut your hair and press your clothes. People will think you are still working. Use your dress and attitude to get you into free happy-hour rooms at convention centers. Carry a name tag, or several of different designs. Use someone else's name. Sometimes, a brass name tag will indicate your exalted rank to the uninitiated.

Discounts: Ask for a discount, no matter where you go. Ask at ticket booths and stores. Ask in restaurants, at shows, even in church. Don't ask at funerals or weddings, or you'll blow your cover.

Seminars: Investment houses and insurance men often will hold seminars with a lunch included. Go, and eat hearty. Do not buy anything. You may want to sign up for a consultation, but call later and cancel. Put down someone else's phone number. Take the sugar, jelly, napkins, mints, pencils, pads, pens, folders, etc. Do not take the silver as it probably belongs to the clubhouse where the lunch is held, and you may be back there at the next lunch.

That's about I have to offer for now. If I come up with anything else, I will include it in my seminar. By the way, I won't have any lunch, mints, pencils, pads, sugar, folders, jelly, or pills, and I may hold my seminar outside, in the park, in the summer. Bring an umbrella.

The Retiree—February, 2004—Blowing

Apologies to those folks living on the north and east sides of the lake. It was inadvertent on my part, but there's no way I can tell who was affected individually. What happened was not entirely my fault, of course (nothing is ever entirely my fault from my perspective), but I must apologize anyway.

Maybe it was mostly my wife's fault. That would be a good way to dodge responsibility. After all, she was complicit in the decision to take care of the dog for five years while our daughter and family are out of the country. And she's the one who wanted a path around the house.

What I did was to blow snow through the dog's favorite area of the yard, to the side of the house, where I decided I was tired. In the process, I discovered maybe one long ton of frozen dog droppings.

Dog droppings sound a little like pine cones when they hit the blades of the blower, except that they don't break up. They evidently soar, and in some cases take a backspin like a Titleist. There's no telling where they will end up, unless they are intercepted by the garage or the house. I directed most of them elsewhere.

While I was blowing spring surprises to various yards, my mind wandered to some tips for snow blower operators that are needed to make it through a Minnesota winter. For example:

—Always run the blower at top speed. Mine won't run any other way anyhow, but doing so will aid in spring yard clean-up for you. Maybe not for your neighbors.

—Before starting your job, run the blower for awhile. In my case, fifteen minutes seems to be right. The township snowplow operator must be able to hear all snowblowers, and when he thinks you have finished the job, he will come by and plow the end of your driveway shut. Waiting fifteen minutes not only warms up my blower, but he plows the driveway shut before I get to the end of the driveway with my blowing.

—Replace brass shear pins in the rotor with steel ones. Chances are the thing won't bend the shaft when a rock gets stuck because the motor will be so weak after a year or so that it will just stop dead. Replacing the brass pin every other snowfall is just too much work. Or, pick up all the rocks. That'll never happen in my case.

—Keep oil on hand. I don't know where it goes, but my stock is always gone, and how can I go get more when the driveway isn't open?

—Save a clean patch of snow upwind. At the end of your job, blow it into the wind. Nothing is more impressive to a wife than to see her husband come in tired and covered with snow. She'll think you have been working your head off. It's refreshing, too.

I hope the above tips help you with your snow relocation processing. You can't just leave the stuff to melt. There's something intriguing and invigorating about the smell of exhaust, the thrill of a blast of cold snow down your neck, the thud of dog droppings against the garage wall. It's all part of the joy of Minnesota living. Enjoy yourself.

The Retiree—February, 2004—Tests

To be retired is to be a little sick. Or maybe a lot sick. To find out which, you have to go to the doctor, because doctors in the aggregate know all things, and you don't.

Some doctors personally don't know all things, so they send you to other doctors who know how to find out all things. This they do through tests with exotic and inscrutable names, always reduced to acronyms, and always involving expensive machines. Examples: MRI's, CTScans, Xrays, BBQs, FBIs, RSVPs.

I went through a battery of such tests. The expensive machines were run by silent young strong women with serious demeanors, who dutifully make charts or whose machines produce charts of their own, none of which can be understood by me. Each machine had its own baffling noise to disorient the one being "machined," namely, me.

Doctors reviewed the results of tests and then did a few of their own, usually requiring disrobing in order to reduce the chances that the victim, or patient, I, would escape. Since my particular problem involved a pinched nerve (I couldn't raise one arm), disrobing was inconvenient at best. Such things are sensed by the silent young strong women, by the doctors, and by any bystanders. A pack mentality takes over. The strong converge to destroy the weak. Here's the process:

Take off your shirt. And your t-shirt. And your pants, come to think of it. (OK.) I'll be back in a minute. (Slam goes the door. Chilly in here.

He comes back.) Hmmm. Is that stethoscope cold? (You bet.) Cough. Breathe in. Hold it. Hmmm. Put your clothes back on and go out and wait for the silent young strong woman. (Slam again. Oof. Putting the shirt on is hard. My arm hurts. Oof oof oof. There, I got the dang thing on again.)

Hi. Step in here. Take off your shirt. And your shoes. (Oof. Oof oof oof. There. That thing is cold, too.) Hmm. I'll get the doctor. You can put on your shirt and shoes. (Slam.) (OK, but I ain't tying my shoes.) Step over to the other office down the hall and wait for that silent strong young woman with your chart. (Oof oof oof oof. There. I'll button my sleeves. Oof oof oof.)

Step over here for an x-ray. Take off your shirt. (Oof oof oof dang buttons oof oof.) The machine may be a little cold. (You bet it is.) Put your chin on here and let me crank it up until your feet come off the floor. Why aren't your shoes tied? I'll go out of the room and get safely into the lead chamber while I send deadly rays through your body. Breathe in and hold it for a day or two. All right, you can exhale and put your shirt on. And tie your shoes. (Oof oof oof oof. I'm buying moccasins.) Here's a cup and there's the bathroom. Read the chart on the wall and put the cup behind the metal door. You know what to do. Leave your shirt on. (Slam.) (Oof. Zippers aren't easy to use when your arm isn't working. I need a whole new set of habits. The metal door is cold. I wonder who else used that handle? I'll wash up. Water's cold, too.)

I made it. I put on my jacket (oof oof oof oof) and headed for my car. Good thing I don't have a manual shift. Not much strength left in that arm. Fortunately, all I had left to do was to have an operation. That would be a cinch. Someone else will take care of my sleeves. Maybe it'll be a silent strong young woman.

The Retiree—February, 2004—Hospitals

I had my operation. Want to see my scar?

Hospitals are a hoot. Laugh, laugh, laugh. The night after my operation I gathered a number of basic truths from the goings-on around me. Some of these truths are remembered from a prior operation but they still hold true. At least most of them are true. You can pick out the truths that are false on your own.

There is no such thing as bedtime in a hospital. Someone is always watching and hatching a plan just for you, a diabolical plan to keep you awake all night. Get your sleep in the daytime. I slept in the afternoon, after the operation, when I felt rotten enough to send my wife home.

A crew of people will show up in the night to throw stainless steel pots down a concrete stairwell somewhere within earshot. This activity will end around two o'clock, when the crew will gather up the pots and argue loudly about who will take them back to the kitchen.

A person claiming to be a nurse will appear at midnight, at two, at two-thirty, at three, and at five, because she is lonesome. She will take your vitals, which are things that plug your ears, disrupt your tongue, and make your arm numb. She will not tell you her findings.

Another patient will go crazy from some of the above causes and will rant and rave for about half an hour, and will repeat the rant at least twice during the dark.

Someone will come in to straighten your bed. It will end up worse, as she will likely make one of your attached tubes bleed, and the sheet will have to be changed.

Everything beeps all night long in the hospital. Beeps in a long series mean the IV is running low, and there is always an IV. A beep in the hall means they want someone, usually the one working on you, to go somewhere else. Other beeps mean the phone is ringing but no one's there to answer, the guard is needed somewhere, a machine is done printing something, coffee's ready, the change machine is out of quarters, someone got really sick, or someone stepped on a pull toy in the lobby. There's a beep machine on your table so you can beep back.

A stentorian voice will bellow for someone named Livingston over a loudspeaker located in the ceiling of your room. The voice will repeat another really long name later. Always a long name. My surgeon's name was Ho. He didn't get paged. This voice also announces that a part of the hospital's computer system is down. And it announces when it comes up. No one cares, least of all the patients.

Someone will ask at four in the morning if you want something to eat or drink. You won't.

For all this, you or some insurance plan is paying many hundreds of dollars for you to sleep. They get their money whether you sleep or not. Maybe that's the solution. The rule should be no sleep, no pay. I'm tired.

The Retiree—March, 2004—Trip

Trips, required for retirees, are sometimes impromptu. Someone calls with a good deal, and you pack too many clothes, pick up two more retirees, and take off in the Buick (most retirees have a Buick). Two of us were recovering from operations and needed respite from boredom. The Buick was white, like an ambulance, appropriately. The destination was Florida, typical for retirees. The trip was made memorable by the people we met. Comments below are true enough for a column.

Our route avoided Chicagoland, always a good idea. We arranged to leech off friends for a night, another good idea. Use friends who have better friends in your home area, so they won't land on your doorstep later. We need friends in Alabama for another stop, but few people retire there. Friends should be 600 miles apart on the road for optimum leeching.

As we prepared to leave Illinois I sat on a coffee cup in the car. Leather seats and black pants reduced the consequences. Coffee rings on underwear don't show, and discomfort is minimal and short-lived. It's part of the travel experience.

A skinny waitress along the Atlantic shore said she was sick and disappeared fror awhile, but managed to show up at tip time. The meal was good, although we weren't sure who would bring the next item. We didn't catch her disease.

Christina at one of Mickey's resorts unburdened herself of all her worldly cares as she took our lunch order. Seems that her stepson had landed on her doorstep again and was causing her great stress and anxiety. She wasn't particularly fond of his companionship. We were treated to a summary of life in a blended household, followed by thanks for listening and a pretty good lunch. She felt better. Not sure that we did.

At Ozzie's Crab Shack we met a gentleman in the parking lot who had been generously overserved on strong beverages. He was moving to Florida from Long Island. He said that his old Buick would beat BMWs in top speed, gratifying as his Buick was older than ours. He agreed that the two planets we were seeing were Venus, Mars, Saturn, and Jupiter, depending on his audience, and smiled and waved pleasantly as we left.

In a motel breakfast room, Bubba from Kentucky told us he'd nearly been sucked into a dam while fishing for 60 lb. catfish, and that his son was in the slammer for bouncing checks. He was grateful to be alive, and was willing to share his life story with anyone who'd listen. We listened for a considerable time. His family had a history of child abuse that covered four generations, but he was willing to let it stop with his son. Seemed like a good idea to us.

One of our goals for the trip was to find manatees. Mickey Mouse's helpers sent us to a state park where a crazy lady was tending the gate. She confronted us with a "what are *you* doing here" attitude, announcing that manatees didn't make reservations, and told Chuck, the driver, to drive next to her yellow lines, not those yellow lines that he'd chosen. He suggested that she should jump in the lake, or more properly, the river. We left, manateeless.

Later, at a local lagoon, six manatees showed up. Some locals rewarded them with bunches of greenery so we wouldn't have to break the no-feeding rules.

Our dog's vacation at the kennel cost more than ours. Now we get to rest up for the next opportunity. No one said retirement would be easy.

The Retiree—April, 2004—Dental

The other day, while eating jellybeans, I discovered that one bean was hard and gold. Simultaneously, I found that one of my upper teeth didn't have a match below. Three hours later, my friendly local neighborhood dentist had drilled a hole completely through the old tooth and into my billfold. She (this one was a she, as the 'he' partner was off investing in offshore tax shelters) stuffed the hole with golf ball covers and old tennis shoes and invited me to return in a couple weeks with more money, which I am duty-bound to do, as I haven't yet completed my home dentistry course.

My first visit to this office years ago was because I'd lost a crown. In ten minutes it had been reattached with some white glue. It cost me eight bucks, if I remember right.

That dental office is now nicely appointed with Persian rugs, crystal chandeliers, designer chairs, marble tables, and every known electronic device. When I started going there, the office was in an old filling station, the grease rack was used for a chair, and a Dremel tool and spackle were used for filling teeth. There was no moat, no flying buttresses, no uniformed guard, no heliport.

Having friends in the same retiree generation, after my appointment I drove quickly to the local volunteer station to find out if the extortion being foisted on me was within reasonable limits. I found that it was, perhaps because of price-fixing, or maybe reflecting prices in the local yacht market. I also found that my companion in misery who was also in the midst of a root canal had to wait for her dentist, who is spending some time frolicking in the British Isles. Some retirement rules have evolved out of this experience, which I gladly share with my grey-haired or no-haired companions.

1. Select dentists as you do surgeons, on the basis of their hands. The smaller and steadier, the better. If large and steady, reject in favor of small and unsteady.

2. Ask about the boat. If the dentist has a multi-engined boat, look elsewhere.

3. Look for antiques in the office. If they became such after the dentist started, fine, but if they are recent acquisitions, check further.

4. Attractive, genial office help is suspect. How did they get happy? Good pay. Look for old crotchety hags with similarly old telephone systems, not touch-screen computers. Frankly, if I were a dentist, I'd hire babes who could use a touch-screen, but I'm not.

5. Check on skill. How? I don't know. Once they start on you, it's too late anyhow.

I know I shouldn't complain. If the dentist wants to complain about me, I guess I can take it. Maybe he thinks Y2K consultants were overpaid. Fine. Frankly, so do I, but I got through the criticism, didn't I? And in good humor, too.

The painful part is over now. If I have to suffer for this column when I go back to finish my root canal, I will simply offer to pass out more jellybeans at the volunteer station. That'll get me in good with them, and will get them more business than they can handle.

The Retiree—April, 2004—Trains

On the way home from the Big City, we see trains heading to and from places west and north of Maple Lake. One can only imagine the contents of all those trains. Some of the cars have Chinese characters on them, some are American with graffiti, and some of them have Canadian characters, eh?

What can be so important as to require a whole train? Well, the Big City has three million people milling around, doing work things, eating meals, driving back and forth, making money. I thought of a few critical items.

Three million people need a lot of rolls of perforated paper. In our home the two of us—and the dog—use maybe two rolls of perforated paper, or TP, a week. We use TP to clean glasses, wipe up dead bugs, blow noses, celebrate events, and provide a means of cleaning in the bathroom that I won't detail. That means the Big City, presuming that people there have the same needs, would use 150 million rolls of TP a year, more or less. Train containers are pretty big, but it's likely that one train running back and forth would be needed just to bring in enough TP to keep the people clean and happy. People with kids, people with cats, and "bunchers" instead of "folders" increase the consumption a lot. Our household has a buncher and a folder. Children love those paper rolls. They take great delight in cramming as much paper in the toilet as possible. One or two children could easily use 100,000 rolls of paper a year, given the freedom to do as they wished.

Then there's noodles. How many noodles are used up in just one Italian or Chinese restaurant in a year? Half of them get thrown away, but they still need a train to bring them in from wherever they make them. I once watched a Chinese noodle-maker in Melbourne, Australia (that's a way of bragging about my travels before my third retirement), as he stretched dough into 2, 4, 8, 16, 32, 64, 128, 256, 512, and maybe even 1024 noodles in a fantastic display of endurance. We were so impressed that we stayed for more green tea, or was it plum wine, and ate noodles in abundance. If that dinner was any indication, there must be a noodle train weekly. How the noodles get from China to Minnesota or Montana or wherever is beyond the scope of this article.

And hopper cars full of coal. Whether they are being shipped to Montana or shipped to Minnesota is beyond me. What is done with it? I think it's made into electricity, but when I look around my meter or outlets or even the computer, there's no sign of coal. I don't understand a lot of those things. It must take a lot of coal to make electricity. I've seen the big piles at the plants around here. Maybe they make coal from electricity, and then ship it out. I spent my career in insurance and consulting, and didn't have to worry about those things. There must be a couple trains a week just shuttling coal back and forth.

Somebody must collect empty boxcars to pick up grain, or autos, or canned goods, or whatever. In college I took a transportation class we called Trains 1 (before they called it Trains 101). The professor smoked a cigarette in a holder. There was a Uniform Freight Classification for horse urine. Those two things were all that I learned in that class. Maybe if I'd paid attention, I'd have been employed by some Montana railroad to find grain cars, and maybe I'd still be working. Maybe. But it wouldn't be as much fun as making up my own facts.

The Retiree—May, 2004—Exigencies

While trying to make a car backup warning system out of a stud finder and some duct tape, my mind wandered to thoughts of the many pressing and difficult problems with which retirees have to deal. Luckily, retirees have been fortified by experience to deal with exigencies and emergencies, especially those of a medical nature.

Everyone I know seems to need some holes cut. Here's a chronicle of what happened just recently. Five days after my fusion operation we went to Florida with A who just had quadruple bypass surgery, and B who was about to have a root canal but didn't know it. We visited C who had to come back to Minnesota for emergency back surgery. D fell out of a tree (why was a 69-year-old up a tree?) and he's recuperating at home with pain pills and a broken back. A just reported that he's about to start chemo and radiation for a colon tumor. Then we heard that E had an uncontrolled nosebleed and made a $1300 ambulance trip to Bemidji from Leech Lake; back trouble, supremely elevated blood pressure. F did a high-speed emergency room run for G. H is having polyps removed from his throat. F had a tooth crown break off and in another quick run got it re-glued. J (I had to skip I because it wasn't me) dropped over on the tennis court and ended up with a bypass. All this in the past few weeks. Some days I don't think we're going to get out of this alive. Sit still, take two aspirin, drink plenty of water and call the doctor in the morning. Whew.

The other problems don't seem to be as critical after dealing with all that cutting and splinting and dashing around. For example, our high-speed loaner dog needs to lean in on the corners in order to make her scheduled arrivals at the bedroom window (bird feeder) and porch window (cat route) and has left black skid marks on our white walls. She's too tall to corner well, but is a demon on the straightaway. I'm researching innovative ways to cover the damage while not straining my neck, and I found the solution. Plastic corners. People make things to solve problems. All one has to do is find them. For another example, step-mother needs help cleaning her apartment. We found a robotic vacuum cleaner that wanders aimlessly around the house, cleaning whatever it pleases. It's very entertaining. Also expensive. If step-mother doesn't buy it, we have a new way to slow down the dog, at least until she decides it's no threat. Another problem dealt with, at least temporarily.

Retirees don't come to life's situations unprepared. We've been there before. The past has equipped us to deal with practically anything. We've missed planes, fixed flats, negotiated settlements, bought houses, shot game, fallen out of boats, eaten squid, hit ourselves with axes, fallen down stairs, broken glasses, woofed cookies, cut fingers, deleted files, set fire to shoes, sold stock at a loss, junked cars, caught skates in cracks, been fired, fired people, made pancakes, been hired, hired people, served as pall bearers, greeted newborns, cut down trees, skidded into ditches, blown up dynamite, given reports, read reports, cleaned fish, prayed, and been prayed for.

Not that I've done any of that, but I can find people who have. That's the advantage of age. Maybe it's the only one.

The Retiree—Memorial Day 2004

"Mom, the lady in the doll store cried when she told me about her house. It got bombed in World War Two." Big lesson for an eight-year-old. Sixty years had passed, and the lady couldn't hold back the tears.

Stuttgart got to me. We found ourselves on top of Birkenkopf, Birch Head, or Rubble Hill, depending on your language and point of view. It's not far from European Command headquarters, where our son was stationed when called up for the war on terrorism.

The view from the top was beautiful. Stuttgart lay spread out beneath us. Cars were zipping down the Autobahn, people were working at the Mercedes plant, hustle and bustle was everywhere. Except on somber, silent Birkenkopf.

Back in the fifties the remains of Stuttgart, 45% destroyed in World War II, were trucked up a small mountain to make a larger mountain. A million and a half cubic meters of rubble were piled randomly and a steep pathway was created to give visitors a glimpse of the past. Lintels bearing addresses stuck out of the ground. Pillars from impressive homes lay exposed. Blocks of stone lay where they were trucked. Church arches poked up from the rocks. One or two stone markers told the story of what happened sixty years ago in that industrial German city.

That memorial in Germany was unusual to Americans, and a little uncomfortable. It called to mind the disaster the country brought upon itself by following an evil leader. It made me think of the suffering of thousands in that lovely, busy place. It made me think of soldiers with no political agenda, simply trying to protect home and family, dying for an evil cause. And it made me think of people huddled in stone cellars, listening to the roar of bombers, hearing the explosions, feeling the shock waves, smelling the acrid smoke. We stood on the remains of the city, on top of the ball bearing plants that were destroyed to shorten the war. And we stood on the house of the lady in the doll store, on her shop, on her church, on her grocery store.

Our victory was good, and sure, and important, and benefited both victor and vanquished. We mourn especially our own in our memorials. But there, on the grounds of the vanquished, on top of that mountain of rubble, were no calm graveyard, no tended garden, no honored flag. All that stood on those broken stones was one tall steel German cross. Alone, silent, it seemed to say, God forgive us. God don't let us ever do this again. God save us from ourselves and from our human foibles.

Standing there, you look at the remains of the devastation, your throat tightens, you suck in your breath, and you say a silent prayer. God, don't let this happen again, anywhere.

That's what Memorial Day is. Happy Memorial Day.

The Retiree—June, 2004—Science

Science is all messed up. Example: Noses continue to grow throughout life, and hair eventually disappears. Arms and legs become less useful. People deteriorate inevitably to a point where they look like bottlenosed dolphins. If science could introduce us to deep salt water, perhaps beginning at retirement, maybe we could eventually join those creatures in the ocean, around Miami Beach or the Bahamas. That wouldn't be all bad, and it could disprove the theory of evolution, presuming that bottlenosed dolphins are lower than humans in the scheme of things, and I believe they are. Most retirees seem to end up someplace near the ocean anyway, and the cost of assisted living would be reduced. Think about it.

Another evidence of the demise of science is my little computer. A couple years ago it was my big computer. It has become my little computer through no action on my part whatsoever. My original computer was state-of-the-art in 1994. It suffered the same fate as my present computer, with no action on my part. People would send me photos, and I would watch the world in the corner of the screen spin for forty minutes. In exasperation I would shut it off, and when I started it up again, it would spend another forty minutes on the photo, which when finally opened, would be of someone's dog, or of something obscene. I had to buy a new computer in order to get messages promptly, just so I could delete them. I still get the same messages. All this is evidence of the decay of science. It also is evidence that programmers insist on using the latest technique, no matter how complicated, to do the simplest tasks. Computer science will eventually deteriorate into a yellow pad and a Ticonderoga #2 pencil with a chewed-off eraser. Watch for this to happen.

Television is another example of the deterioration of things scientific. When I was in high school and my parents finally bought a television set, there was one channel, and we watched whatever was on it, and thought it was great. Come to think of it, Sid Caesar and Imogene Coca and I Remember Mama and Ed Sullivan were great. Now we have fifty or a hundred channels with nothing to watch, except someone building a motorcycle or painting a room.

All the important stuff was invented long ago. Consider the wheel, the toothbrush, power outside mirrors, the hole in the toilet seat, fire, minnow bucket oxygen tablets, smokeless powder, synthetic eggs. What more do we need?

Did you ever really look at a brace and bit, or a scythe, or an oarlock, or a block plane? Elegant simplicity. Those things worked well, and didn't have to be plugged in or use gasoline. And we think we've progressed because we get ads on the internet for sex gadgets from some teen-aged pervert in Holland. Those teen-aged perverts should be locked up and made to use manual sod-kickers for 20 years, but that's another topic.

Come to think of it, just what was my topic, anyway? I'm staring out the window instead of working my muscles to avoid turning into something like the little bronze statue of the goose girl on our shelf in the living room. You don't need me to remind you of the cornball world we live in. Have a nice day. As they say, we're all in this together.

The Retiree—June, 2004—Roofs

Finally I figured out how to fix the leaks in our roof. I hired a roofer to put on a new one.

Up to this time I've tried a variety of stopgap measures such as denying the problem, putting towels on the floor, saying that was a 100-year storm, putting up eaves troughs, using old roofing tar from the basement antique-fluids storehouse, and diverting water with an angle iron. Nothing worked if the rain was over 1.8 inches. Less than that, it wouldn't leak. Why the limit was 1.8 inches was never determined.

The dog spent the day with her ears laid back. She told us repeatedly that there were people on our roof, and she couldn't understand why we didn't chase them off. Her loss of confidence in our judgment was palpable. Nobody would obey her herding commands. If that little brain is programmed to herd things together, and the things continue to wander around, including climbing onto the roof, what's a dog to do? Don't ask me. I couldn't solve her problem.

Our house was built in 1951 and 1957 and 1964 and 1996, if I remember correctly. Shingles generally followed that schedule, except for maybe 1992 when a really bad patch job was done and we had to hurry back to South Carolina. When contractors would ask if there was more than one layer of shingles up there, I'd have to say yes, no, maybe one or two or three, or none in some places.

We've taken fairly good care of the place, outside of that. A river (the rivers are only active during rains) no longer runs through the basement, and most of the west river has been diverted to a confluence with the east river by an extension of the downspout. No new cracks have been noticed in what's left of the foundation. There's insulation all over the place except for the 1964 windows, and we're thinking about fixing them. We don't have an outdoor toilet now. We have a furnace that works. There's a driveway instead of a trail. Most of the Plains Indians in the 1860s lived in more primitive conditions than we now have, which was not the case in 1996.

After the roofer suppressed a look of desperation, he announced that he couldn't add more vents to our roof, since there seemed to be another roof under the one he was roofing. That was no news to us, having seen the 1951 through 1964 iterations of the structure. We saw a similar look of desperation once on the face of a contractor who was denying that one of our walls was a bearing wall. Hah. That wall bears the old roof. Surprises go along with old cabins.

City folks have complications that we don't have. We don't have strangers driving up and down our road. We don't have sirens and buses and taxicabs. We don't have neighbors six feet from our kitchen. While the dog was barking and the roofers were laying waste to our plantings, we could still look out on Maple Lake and watch the loons and listen to the soft cooing of outboard motors. We did, after all, need a roof. So, in spite of the crushing load of debt we are incurring, we still love it here.

The Retiree—July, 2004—Kids

Our shower emits a squeal from time to time. To make it quit, I pull up on the spout shower button. I found that by careful manipulation of the button, I can make the spout play the first few notes of "Take the A-Train." By happy chance I have found the basis for a new jazz medium. Admittedly the space for performance is small, only one seat, but a lot of jazz venues are small, and are usually called "intimate." What could be more intimate than a bathroom? This project will be difficult, but what worthwhile things aren't? I can only emerge cleaner, so the effort won't be wasted in any case. I need to find my old Artie Shaw and Benny Goodman records, and the LP record player, to study up a little so I can branch out into Swing. Imagine "Begin the Beguine" on a bathtub spout. I'd never have time for this if I had a job. Lately I haven't had any time even though I'm retired. Here's why.

While waiting for my chance at fame in the world of jazz, we've been entertaining our St. Lucian daughter and family. I just sat down at the computer after putting the two-year-old to bed. Again. Next to the computer. The deal was I'd sit here until his mom comes home if he'd lie down. Seemed fair at the time, but I may have to write a novel. My bedtime story didn't have any effect. I found some good reading in the Wall Street Journal, but once I'd read the yearly highs and lows to him for some pretty fascinating stocks, he seemed to lose interest. Happened last night, too. I think I'll try Barron's. They have some good editorials.

Yesterday our Lucians had a little get-together with every fruitful member of their various past schools and affiliations. We had 19-8/9 children under age eight here. Every family required a van or Suburban. We want to thank those who helped us through the crisis until we regained enough nerve to go home again. Nothing got busted except for one pot, and I busted that. You'd have busted something, too; don't tell me you wouldn't.

Breakfast has been interesting. First out is the five-year-old. She wants toast, jelly no butter, not warmed up (that means bread). Next is the seven-year-old, toast on setting one, butter, jelly. Next is the dad, who wants coffee. Dog comes next, who wants out. Some variation in sequence and diet occurs for the remaining members. We don't have breakfast in bed any more. There is no routine for the rest of the day. We will miss all that when they leave.

The dog thought about showing her teeth to the two-year-old once. We told her she gets no free bites. One bite and she's out. She looked discouraged, tried to negotiate, but finally gave in. Today she licked the two-year-old in the face, indicating complete submission. That's a relief. Maybe we'll give her a free shot at the FedEx man as a reward.

I think the two-year-old went to sleep. Now I can sneak out, and wonder where his mom is. She has to come back. She's got my car.

The Retiree—August, 2004—Music

Every morning, no matter how early I can't sleep any more because of various aches and pains, I wake up with a song running through my head. Some days it's Brahm's Lullaby in German (although I only know the first line and am not German), some days it's a medley by Oscar Peterson, some days it's 99 Bottles of Beer on the Wall, some days it's exerpts from Handel's Messiah. It could be anything. Maybe Heart and Soul on the piano by a couple of pre-teen girls. A shower sometimes clears the player. Breakfast or the radio will make the song go away, or at least change it.

There's no way to control the music. It seems to be an involuntary thing, like sweating or belching. I don't know who's in charge. My mother-in-law, who had songs running through her head in the middle of the day, thought it was the devil, but he seems to be too busy in the Mideast to bother with my internal CD player. She'd have been okay with Brahms or Handel, but I suspect that 99 Bottles would have confirmed her suspicions as to the identity of the disc jockey in her head.

I don't plan to do anything to make the songs go away. Psychoanalysts or counselors wouldn't help, I'm sure, and besides I can't afford to support any more boats for medical people. It's better entertainment than those drive-time radio people who by virtue of their employment have become expert in international relations or investments, and I can listen without having to turn the volume up or down.

Maybe the music is a substitute for those dramatic thoughts that used to wake me when I was employed. I don't have to worry about Louise suing the company for age discrimination, or Dick thinking I would be finished with that test replay that somehow didn't start because the network went down, or Fred running a status request that used 4 boxes of paper. I don't have to think about buying gas on the way to work and being late, or getting caught in traffic. Budgets and complaints and calling irate people are distant memories.

Here's my theory. At retirement, the brain gathers up all those concerns over important things that have suddenly become irrelevant, and it tosses them down one's throat, to be digested and eliminated. That leaves a big hole in the brain that has to be filled. The brain looks around for things that weren't very important in the past, and it tucks them away in that open space. For me, and I suspect for a lot of retirees, the space is perfect for expanding CDs and vinyl 33s and old 78s that it formerly had to hold in some sort of packed format because of all that important stuff. Thus, the theme music from Lucy and Desi, steel pan songs from the Caribbean, campfire singing, and old rotten Jody cadence from basic training are all put in condition for instant replay, triggered by waking up.

I'd like to do a formal paper on my theory, but that would be a little too time-consuming. Right now, I'm busy trying to remember the second verse of America the Beautiful. It's in my brain's storage someplace, probably where my airplane schedule for that trip to Omaha used to reside. That's my theory, and I'm sticking to it.

The Retiree—August, 2004—Parties

Dock parties are great fun. We try to horn in on them whenever possible.

One of their great benefits is to provide us with some insight about who is related to whom. In the past, we've been embarrassed to find that the person or persons we were verbally maligning were related to the person or persons to whom we were confiding. For example, we might say to B that we were following someone who turned into A's driveway after they swerved to run over a cat, and B would say yup, A's my uncle, and he hates cats, and I'll tell him you watched as he ran over the cat. So, it's a real benefit to be able to find out that not only is A related to B, but C who lives by the channel is related to A by marriage, and the only thing he hates more than cats is people who hate people who hate cats.

Another benefit to the parties is that we can get a new vantage point on the lake. We can see who can see our house, who can see into our house, and just how insignificant our house looks from over there. We can see that we've got to trim that tree, and we need to paint the door, since it looks like someone barfed on it. We can tell which windows need shades, and we can tell people that we live next to that nice house but you can't see the best part of ours because of the trees. Places on the lake can't be identified easily from the road anyway, and once the people get home, they'll forget which house was ours, and also what our names were, with any luck at all. One of our secrets is to write our names illegibly on name tags.

A third benefit is that whoever gave the party usually has a bunch of goodies just begging to be eaten. If you're early enough, you can grab the ones with the most frosting and leave the fruit for late-comers. Enough coffee is normally there to wake you up, and there may be enough to encourage an early departure, unless the house is open for tours and you can find a bathroom.

If we should ever be so careless as to have a dock party at our house, we will stipulate that attendees bring a paint brush or shovel. That'll keep the crowd down. We will have refreshments, but we won't have napkins, and we'll have weak coffee in paper cups without handles. We may have juice, but it will be from concentrate and we won't stir it. The dog will be loose. We won't have enough parking space; our vehicles will be outside and we will lock the garage. The bathroom doors will be locked, too. We will have name tags but no pens. We will be quite friendly, though, so people will think our omissions were inadvertent. That should take care of any future parties.

Many thanks to those who are genuinely cordial and who have those wonderful dock parties where we gain all those insights about the neighbors. We don't know what we'd do without them. One thing's clear. We'd probably have to buy our own doughnuts and coffee.

The Retiree—August, 2004—Teeth

"Over eight hunnert beans for a tooth? Them guys is nuts. Here at Dick's Fast Lube and Tooth Repair we oughta be able to do it for maybe 30, 40 bucks. Have a seat in this barber chair. You don't need a haircut too, do you? I can give you a break on the price." The proprietor was very self-assured.

I came here too spontaneously, I thought. I hoped he'd washed his hands after changing oil in that '78 Chev. But with the savings, I should be able to buy a few aspirins and some alcohol. Maybe a couple kinds of alcohol.

"Bernice, Bernie for short, will be helping. She used ta be a dental person until that thing about malpractice or malfeasance or maladjustment or whatever. She knows her way around mouths, though. So what's the problem, then?" Dick asked, trying to look concerned, in his best dental mode.

I complained about the estimate I'd got at the dentist's office. I showed it to him, with the diagram of which tooth was bad. It was an old root canal and I told him that I'd feel no pain in it.

"Hah! We'll see if ya feel no pain!" was the reassuring response. "Bernie, get the air wrench. This looks like a booger ta me."

Bernie responded, and on the way back with the air hose picked up a plastic grocery bag from the magazine rack. In it were some pretty impressive dental tools, along with a couple peanut butter sandwiches and an apple. She handed one of the tools to Dick; at least I think it was Dick, as he never introduced himself. "Here's a probe," she said.

"Ya, tell him to wait. Is it that guy with the '91 Probe? I just changed his oil last week," Dick responded.

"No, this pointy thing for the tooth is the probe. Dig around and see how loose that old crown is. Maybe we won't need the air wrench, except for drying out the hole we make."

Bernie began stuffing cotton in my mouth and announced that we'd need a couple impressions. Dick pointed to the rubber cement on the oil filter shelf and asked Bernie where that spackle was. Bernie grabbed the air hose and shot a blast into my mouth, popping my ears and blowing my cheeks out like a balloon. I was dried out instantly.

"Looks a little loose to me," announced Dick. "Got a vise grip?"

"Use the Dremel tool. It's got a cutting wheel on it. Careful of his tongue, though. You know how hard it is to understand Sweeney now that you fixed his bridge."

Dick gave a couple cranks on the barber chair and positioned his foot on my chest. He fiddled with the cutting tool attachment and pried my mouth open.

As I sped out of the shop, the Dremel tool was still in my mouth. I spit it out onto the driveway as I spun away and headed back toward the dentist's office. Seems that some things are just plain worth the cost. Not sure about the haircut, though. Could be a deal.

The Retiree—September, 2004—Sales

Garage Sale. Those words strike terror in the hearts of many a husband. Moving Sale brings more trepidation to those who are retired and are called upon to accompany wives on their daunting rounds. Our neighbors added depth to those frightening epithets with a sale that transcends either Garage or Moving: The House Burning Sale (HBS). Yes, they are burning their house down. Or, rather, the fire department is going to burn their house down.

Neighbors arranged the burning in order to build Their Retirement Home (TRH). That's what happens here on the lake. People do away with old places and replace them with new places, using the excuse that the foundation caved in, or the roof is falling off, or there's no insulation, or we can't afford city taxes and a lake place, or all of the above. Excuses.

We agreed to babysit the House Burning Sale (HBS) for a time while the owners went to the Powers That Be (PTB) to plead for mercy so their floor plan could extend to within inches of the lake, the road, and all of us neighbors. PTB agreed to allow the new structure to be built, providing that the flying buttresses not extend beyond the property line, that the moat be eliminated, that the towers not extend into airport air space, and that colors exclude iridescent reds and purples, regardless of the influence of the Red Hat Club.

While they were gone, we had full command of the cash box, the folding doors, the water heater, the lawnmowers, the carafes, the sets of dishes, the books, the doorknobs, the carpets, the egg candling equipment, the punch presses, the spare wheels, the harpoons, the knee pads, the spice racks, the sweaters, the baseball caps, the cheese graters, the gas tanks, the periscopes, the remote controls, the battle-axes, the seashell lamps, and all the other extraneous stuff (ES) collected carefully over half a century of cabin occupancy.

People of all stripes attended the HBS. Some came in old vans, prepared to haul off ES. Some came in new pickups, showing evidence that they didn't need anything being sold, but just wanted to show off their 4WD on the gravel driveway. Some argued over prices, refusing to pay $2.50 for that Gutenberg Bible, saying they saw one just like it that morning for 95 cents over by Howard Lake. Some hooked together like objects, saying no, the hose and the nozzle weren't separate, and the tag was 40 cents for the whole thing.

Some HBS attendees simply walked off with stuff. We saw you going over the hill with that cast iron pot; don't deny it. The pot was a family heirloom, handed down for ten generations, and certainly worth the $4500 tag on it, and if we could have got that powder and wad stuffed down the genuine antique Tennessee muzzle-loader a little faster, we'd have popped you in the hinder.

Others were nice people, giving us great lumps of money for things that no sensible person would ever be seen with, and for those kind neighbors we give thanks. It takes all kinds. Those running an HBS appreciate people with a good 4WD who buy ES while the owners are at the PTB.

The Retiree—June 22, 2004—Reunion

"Want to go to the 100-year anniversary all-class reunion of my hometown school? And annual town celebration? And carnival? My brother's going but she (his wife) isn't," said my wife. I said I had a date with his wife but could break it. She suggested breaking it, but it looked like she didn't believe me, or she thought at my age I'm harmless.

Events included a pork dinner, prepaid before I had a chance to question whether eating there would be a good idea. The reason for the event was to create a forum for talking. The attendees did so with great exuberance. I've heard those conversations before. They include massive numbers of names. The surnames are familiar to everyone there regardless of graduation year, and apply to married females as well as males. If your great-grandfather was a Klaassen, K with two a's and two s's, your great-grandfather's name will be specified when your first name is used; e.g. "Beatrice Fairweather, Klaassen two a's and two s's," to distinguish her from Beatrice Fairweather, C Clausen, or K Klassen one a two s's, or K Klaasen two a's and one s, just in case more Beatrices existed. I knew that I'd hear all those names, just as I did last time there was a reunion. This time I wouldn't have the support of a sister-in-law to share my blank look.

Here's a sample conversation. I left off quotation marks and names since they only interrupt the flow of words, and in the picnic-table setting when everyone's talking at once, it didn't matter who was saying what anyway.

Is Harvey here? Harvey who? Harvey and his daughter—I saw her and maybe him. Kay was seen—anyone check the register? She wouldn't sign in—she doesn't want anyone to know she's here. Who brought Bubba, the C Clausens? No, Jane did, she's got the wheelchair. Harvey who? Yes, with his daughter. Was Paul at the convocation? Back row, far side. Ever seen so much gray hair? Who's Harvey? Where's the Class of 2000? They don't want to be seen—maybe in ten years. Besides, somebody's got to do the milking. Where you living? Denver, but I just got laid off. Who's got the California Buick? Bald guy, class of '64, football—you'd never know it. Who's Harvey? Yes.

Two convocations were held, separated by a basketball game. The game combined new grads with really old grads, some of whom were seen actually running. Emergency fire and rescue people were preparing for a pancake breakfast, so running was really risky. Firemen said they'd put up a sign announcing that no fires would be permitted until after 1 PM Sunday. Nobody died. Just lucky.

We took a ride around the area. Motorcyclists in the campground were harmless. Each farm driveway was an occasion to stop and wave—there's Jake having a picnic, there's Nick two a's one s having a party, there's the communal farm, fighting amongst themselves now. There's the Indian mound, opened but covered up so someone can find it again in fifty years.

It was exhausting. Dinner was good, if you ate early. I didn't remember many names. Maybe there'll be a 200-year reunion. By then I'll have forgotten the names anyhow.

The Retiree—September, 2004—Wedding

"Let's go to the wedding," said my spouse. "They'd really like some family representation there. His side will have lots of people, and her side won't have anybody. We'll be important to someone again. Someone will hug me. Besides, with few family, we'll be able to sit up front."

"The last time I saw her, she was three. The wedding's in a hayfield up in Muskeg Central, Minnesota. The car will need an oil change. We're broke. What if the weather turns bad? This is the possible snow season. What is a "casual" wedding, anyway? Where did her fiancee get that goony hat in this picture? Why can't your brother go?" I was running out of really good excuses. "I need a haircut. I have a cold. My shoulder hurts. We don't have a gift. Her father wouldn't let me use his paint sprayer. Her mother's remarried and I bet he's a jerk. Someone will make a scene. I don't think I can find the hayfield."

"My sister-in law's going to ride along and share the cost. She bought a gift. And a card. I told her we'd pick her up. Find your casual shoes. The weather's supposed to be fine. There's free beer. The bridesmaids are babes. We'll stop at a casino—or not, if you don't like casinos, and wipe that grimace off your face. We're going." She's persuasive.

We went for the afternoon wedding. The yard was full of cars. First one I saw was a Jaguar. Next to it, a '75 Ford pickup. Then a row of

Buicks, all driven (of course) by septuagenarians. There may have been a tractor or two, but they could have been parked there earlier. The couple's limousine was already parked. It had a brush guard, skid plate, four-wheel drive, and a new topper. Every type of camper filled the yard, parked helter-skelter among the scrub pine and popple. Shots could be heard in the distance; hunters poaching grouse or popping doves off wires. All the folding chairs in Aitkin were lined up facing a trellis loaded with flowers. Port-a-potties were placed discreetly behind the house. A tent worthy of Oktoberfest was anchored to the ground, bowed slightly up and to the north by a respectable wind. Grasshoppers were leaping gaily up pants and skirts.

Every manner of dress was there. Casual means different things to different people. Some wore shorts. Some wore formal gowns. Some wore tuxes. Some wore camo. (The colors for the wedding were blaze orange and camouflage.) City people had cell phones on their belts. Locals had cell phones and Buck knives. There were cowboy boots, hunting boots, farm boots, wing tips, moccasins, sandals, bare feet, high heels, clogs, and one pair of four-inch-thick flip-flops in shocking pink. There was one yellow labrador and a few blackbirds, dressed as is their custom.

Grandpa and a judge conducted the wedding. We think it went off well, but since they were shouting upwind, we didn't hear much. The battery-powered organ didn't fare well, either, as it was drowned out by an acoustical guitar. Someone sang some country songs. We took pictures of the girls as their heels sank into the hayfield. Each member of the bridal party had a body part or two pierced or tattooed. The groom wore that hat. A voice told us to carry our chairs with us to the tent if we expected to sit down to eat. We did.

It's a gutsy thing, having an outdoor wedding in Minnesota. Especially when one of the guests sends columns to the newspaper.

The Retiree—September, 2004—Fire

We put a screen door on the back of our house. Since remodeling, we'd done without one. With the inside door open, the neighbors could see from their porch clear into our vanity where we brush our teeth. Shortly after we added the door, the neighbors burned their house down. Evidently we're not as attractive as we used to be.

The fire was the social event of the season. Everyone who was anyone around the lake was there. They came on foot and in golf cars. Some drove, but parking was at a premium because almost every vehicle in town that was painted red took up the space on the road.

In the past we had opportunities to go to two other similar events, but other commitments had prevented our attendance. This particular event couldn't be avoided. We could almost reach the fire from our driveway with our wiener forks.

Equipment on display from the Maple Lake fire department was impressive. They even brought their kiddie pool. Since it was too chilly for swimming, they stuck their pumper hoses in it. Pumping water from the lake apparently fries too many sunfish, and as the neighbors had brought hot dogs in profusion, we didn't need any fish.

A fireperson climbed on the roof and chopped a hole, releasing a bat, giving credence to the decision to burn the place down. Firepeople cut slots in the corners of the house, to make it fall in instead of out. We were all learning techniques of fire fighting that we'd never use.

A firefellow went around with a torch, lighting fires around and under the house. Weren't firefighters supposed to put those things out, not start them? Smart-alecky remarks abounded. "Your Rolex was still on the dresser," followed by "Tell the insurance company!" This was Smart-aleck Central for an hour or so. Nobody had an unexpressed opinion. We were grateful that the butt of all the comments was a neighbor and not us.

Bottles and cans could simply be thrown on the floor of the house, if one could get close enough to do so. There were a few extra things placed under the porch that didn't belong there, and the firemenandwoman (one gal) also found an opportunity to add to the kindling with odds and ends.

Before I forget, the fire department was very capable. There. That's out of the way.

On a couple occasions, fireguysandgal walked out on the dock and scooped up pails of water. There was ice in the coolers, water in the kiddie pool, hoses galore, but they wanted lake water. I didn't ask why. I'd rather make up some reason of my own.

We set up chairs in our driveway and found that nobody sits down at these events. They cruise around, watching the fire, looking in the windows, watching smoke come out the back door, checking the coolers and hot dogs on the grill. It's a first-rate way to socialize.

We'll be looking for the next house fire. It's a great way to spend an evening. But, a word of caution: DON'T DO IT YOURSELF. The firepeople have much better hoses.

The Retiree—October, 2004—Wedding

Once upon a time there was a wedding in the Big Woods, far from the general populace, in a hayfield where none had ever been married before, save maybe a Chippewa or two. We were among those chosen to attend the wedding. Perhaps you heard about it.

Among the interesting facets of this multi-faceted affair was one facet involving accommodations. There was little near the wedding for accommodating humankind, although there were ample accommodations for animals, wild and domestic. To accommodate those needing accommodations, an accommodation list accompanied the invitation, as did an invitation to bring one's own accommodation in the form of a camper. Getting two senior women to pitch a tent in a hayfield was simply unspeakable, so I didn't speak it. Instead, the sister-in-law, call her Arlene because that's her name, who was to accompany us to the accommodation appointed herself as an accommodation accommodater. She found accommodations only twenty or so miles from the wedding, much closer than going home.

Arlene said it was a little iffy when she called to make reservations, as the accommodation lady seemed to speak only a foreign tongue. The accommodation lady admitted to belonging to a group of motels of good repute; we'll call them Zippy Inns for purposes of this column.

We wondered if Zippy Inns would be able to care for our dog while we went to the hayfield. I called the Zippy Inn number and talked to the accommodation lady who gave me a garbled explanation involving some obscure convention in her society that involved eating dogs, so we decided to leave the dog home. We were going to the noted world-wide Zippy Inn chain, were reassured, and wouldn't need to bring our army surplus shelter halves.

After the wedding, reception, and dance, we drove to the Zippy Inn. But there was no Zippy Inn. There was a Wimpy Inn. We went in and asked where Zippy Inn was. Wimpy Inn had bought out Zippy Inn two years ago. Someone at Wimpy's who spoke fluent English as a first language looked at the invitation and found that most of the accommodations thereon had the same phone number, no matter where they were. She called the Shabby Inn, twelve miles down the road. They had our reservation.

We immediately recognized the accent of the accommodation lady at Shabby Inn. She denied ever saying she was a Zippy Inn member. By this time we were mentally and physically exhausted, so with a quick look at the room, we flipped out a credit card and stumbled into our accommodation.

After killing a grasshopper in the bathroom, stomping a bug in the bedroom, and returning three towels that were hung behind the bathroom door, we collapsed in a stupor until morning, when we had a free breakfast of unmixed frozen orange juice, decaf, and day-old doughnuts.

There is no moral to this story. Nothing can be learned from it. You have just wasted about the same amount of time on it that we spent discussing it afterward. But at least I feel better.

The Retiree—November, 2004—Advice

There's been lots of whining on TV talk shows lately. I'm reminded that people believe what they want to believe, and see what they want to see, regardless of the facts. To combat this process, the world needs an advice column that lays it on the line, calls a spade a spade, and smacks people in the face with information. Guess what. I'm here. Of course, nobody asked me, so I made up the questions. Doesn't every advice columnist do that?

Q. My boyfriend has a '57 Olds that he spends more time with than me. How can I get him to pay attention to me instead of that car?

A. A '57 Olds? Has he got the J-2 engine with 3 2-barrel carbs? Have him call me. I've always wanted to see that progressive linkage in action. I'll bring my own carburetor cleaner.

Q. The election depressed me. How can I cope with an administration that goes counter to everything I hold to be true?

A. Get over it, you twit. You lost. Grow up, or move to Canada, if they'll take you. And bring your own drugs. They'll be shipping all theirs down here.

Q. What's with those walleye slot limits? Why can't I eat whatever I catch?

A. The state legislature is working on a plan where fish will have rulers inscribed on their sides. Just lift them up and read the last number on the tail. No more problems. Anyway, if you like sushi, you can always eat them right there in the boat.

Q. Speaking of fish, didn't the Pope or some bishop tell Senator Kerry to go fish or something? And didn't Bush say he was going to activate churches to do his charitable work?

A. Nobody here elected the Pope. Maybe you should go to church and find out a few things for yourself, instead of whining to me. Who do you think I am? The Archbishop of Canterbury?

Q. Why does the phone ring when I go to the bathroom, and when I pick up, nobody's there?

A. Have you looked out the window instead of answering the phone? Maybe somebody's outside with a cell phone.

Q. How come we can spend $200 billion shooting people in the desert but we can't seem to fix the highways so I can go see my grandchildren without staying overnight?

A. Stop trying to equate things monetarily. If you can explain how the Chinese can make an umbrella out of fifty pieces, pack it in bubble wrap, send it 8,000 miles on a ship, pay a longshoreman to unload it to a truck, send it to a warehouse and then a chain store, hire a kid to hang it on a rack, pay another to chew gum and take your five bucks, and have everyone make money, then I'll tell you about the desert.

Q. Why do people in big new houses on the lake shine spotlights on the water? Why don't they shine them on their houses?

A. Don't ask me. I've got a little old house on the lake.

Well, that was fun, sort of. Maybe I'll do it again some time. Meanwhile, my head is starting to hurt. Just how do they make those umbrellas for five bucks, anyway?

The Retiree—January, 2005—Water

Every day the lake changes. Sometimes it's whitecaps and sometimes it's sunsets and sometimes it's blizzards. Lately it was different because of a gap between the "real" ice and the ice on the layer of water we got from that unseasonable rain awhile ago. The water on top of the ice had a gap of air between it and the top ice. There goes my skating for the year, and I haven't even laced up my skates yet.

The dog found out quickly that the top ice wouldn't support her, and the water between the ice layers was mighty cold, discouraging her stick-chasing. So I threw her stick carefully along the edge of the lake where the ice was one layer, and she agreed to wear herself out there. I threw carefully for her sake, and for mine because last year throwing it with abandon resulted in an operation and I didn't want to do that again.

I grew up in the Big City, close to the Big River, where we were forbidden to go, especially in winter. One winter when we were playing down by the Big River, Paul fell through the ice. He scrambled up again, and we naturally went on with our playing. Paul's dad, knowing that if we weren't in the yard we must be in forbidden territory, found tracks leading to a hole, and didn't see the tracks leading away, so he naturally assumed that we were dead and called out the police and fire department and National Guard and Highway Patrol and most of the clergy in the Big City. When Paul got home, he was greeted by more officials than the Mayor had been greeted with at election time. Paul learned that he should not go to forbidden territory again, and I learned to keep my mouth shut. Another time, Bruce fell through the ice on a small pond in a vacant lot. He was offered heat and dry clothing but opted to walk three blocks home instead. He made it. We all survived to adulthood.

Once we played around a burned-out grain elevator, where there were deep empty bins half filled with water, from which there would be no escape had one fallen in. Always, we played near cold and dangerous water, being kids and rotten swimmers and wanting to scare hell out of our parents. A search party was sent out that time, too, but of course we were home before anyone could find us.

If there's a point to all this, it's that parents in general don't know what kids are up to, and of course as parents in turn we had no idea what our kids were up to. Sooner or later, such as at the groom's dinner when they get married, parents find out a few things. And so do kids. Mine will find out something if they read this. I found out that my dad used to ride the ice floes on the Big River when he was a kid, and he couldn't swim at all, but I didn't find out until he was well into his fifties, when he knew I wouldn't try to replicate his feats.

Key to this is that one should always try to keep one's guardian angel happy. You just don't know when you're going to need him.

The Retiree—January, 2005—AADS

TV reports that there's a new drug on the market for something called Adult Attention Deficit Syndrome. I wonder how you tell if Hey, what's the dog barking at now? She's always running around the house Wasn't ADD something spurious that showed up in grade school kids who didn't want to do the lessons Today I'm going to fix that shade in the bath I gotta call my Chicago cousin soon to see if she'll pick us up

Will the snow blower start next time? Seems like the old gas was the problem Starter fluid has the top knocked off and it will blow Maybe the guy with the plow Ice fishermen seem to take a lot of time off from work.

Where are all the tax reports? They were around here Is this the day when there are dollar hamburgers No, that's Thurs Shouldn't the neighbors be gone to Arizona Just like the swans, they seem to stay around until When is that report going to show up on the History Channel My hammer must be in the basement, not in the garage, and I know I should put up a hook for the broom so it doesn't freeze to the deck again Why should anyone need a drug for—what would they call it—AADD? Sounds like something for alcoholics Why doesn't the cork fit back into the wine bottle when it's been there since it was bottled My sketch pad is around here someplace, and what happened to that new software I ordered last Maybe the mail got held up.

Isn't there a way to order groceries and have them waiting when we get there Shouldn't I wait for my regular dental appointment to check out that Why can't I get more than a month's worth of pills from the drug What is that ADD drug for adults, anyway, and why would anyone want it?

If we're going to get up the hill from the garage, we'd better get some salt How can I get that light switch to stay on until I'm in the If the dog would only go in one place I could clean it up better but she can't even sleep in the same place all night And why were the cops driving an old Bronco anyway? I'd have been suspicious having one follow That last shooting was near my old junior high school; Minneapolis is a changed Should I do something with all that foreign change in the dresser drawer?

Wife's been reading over my shoulder. She just went in to turn on the TV. Said something about finding an ad for a drug she thought I need for paying attention to…whatever.

Right, I should get another drug. We already have a bunch of drugs around. Maybe I should just take a few more of those.

The Retiree—February 2005—Karl

One recent morning we turned on the coffee and the television and the computer to see what was new. We found out that one of the wife's cousins had died. (Call him Karl for this column.) During retirement, more and more the morning drill is to look around and see who woke up. With increasing frequency, there's someone we know who isn't there any more.

Karl was a little atypical of acqaintances we would pick. Being a relative, we didn't have the luxury of picking. Karl felt that things like corporations and free markets and monetary systems and the military were intrinsically evil. He'd express his unconventional views as soon as he met you. "Hello, I'm Karl and I hate capitalists." Although he knew he was in the minority he also knew he wouldn't be really happy until his nemeses all went away. We were surprised that he died from a heart attack, as we'd always thought he would end up being shot by a soldier or run over by a capitalist's limousine. Fortunately he lived in a small prairie college town and could easily dodge those conservatives who came at him in their John Deeres.

We'll miss Karl. People come over to our house and discuss things we concur in, and have no problems with us. We settle in to conversations that aren't memorable at all, and when they leave, we go on drifting comfortably through some sort of ennui. When Karl left, he usually fired off a parting shot, such as "I'll never understand why you voted for Hitler," or something to keep you thinking. That's gone now, and we're sorry.

It's interesting how feelings about people get ingrained in your consciousness over the years. Relative A: Remember how Emma stole the farm from Uncle Oscar? Relative B: No she didn't Oscar gave it to her. Relative C: No he didn't he gave it to Hank and she stole it from him. Relative D: No their dad gave it to Emma and Oscar didn't want it and neither did Hank. Well, thirty years have passed, and D and B still think Emma was wonderful, and there's no way C and A can ever be persuaded that Emma was anything but a conniver. It's that blind Indian and the elephant thing; it's very like a tree trunk / snake / broom / whatever. Some people, though, are what they appear to be and everyone concurs. That was Karl. He wasn't the sort that could be ignored, or misinterpreted. I'd like to be a little more defined, like Karl.

But don't look to me for anti-military or anti-corporate thought. Better to be thought of as a tree trunk, or a broom. Or maybe even a snake.

The Retiree—March, 2005—St. Lucia

Rodney Heights, St. Lucia, West Indies:

We're spending a month here reacquainting ourselves with grandchildren and getting sunburned. Retirees do that, decimating their children's inheritance.

Things move slowly here. Retirees like that, generally. But in the Caribbean, 'slowly' has its own definition. Our son-in-law got an 'overnight' package shipment that was dated 2 months and 24 days earlier. He also got a notification of a February 10 meeting—on March 1. Our 9:30 AM boat ride left promptly at 10:25. Tennis lessons began an hour late. The grade school horseback riding class never did convene. The landlord, who said he'd come before 8, showed up at 9:10. Nobody seems to mind, though.

A page from *The Maple Lake Messenger* showing ice fishing was well received at the grade school, but there were many questioning looks (Trucks on the ice? Ice? Snowsuits? Who ya trying to kid?)

Rodney Bay, down in the high rent district, attracts "yachties" who sometimes regard local conventions with disdain. Down by the harbor we were pushed aside by some Spaniards who were looking for cruise clothing; nearly pushed off the sidewalk by two French tourists; watched some Brits walk by in their swimming suits (a dreadful violation of Lucian dignity). To our relief, no Americans were noticed that time. When we violate local island dignity, we simply fake a

German accent and move along. If we do something right, we sound American and toss of a "bo'-jou" or "bo'swe" to show our love of the culture. It seems to work.

Some people show up at Rodney Bay in boats that are larger than most of the world's navy ships. Apparently they aren't retired, and have never done anything from which to retire. Names painted on their sterns—their boats' sterns, that is—include New Orleans, Boston, Hannover, Marseilles, Florence, Chicago, Martinique (locals, almost), and others. If I had a boat here, I'd paint "South Haven" or "Kimball" on it.

Cruise ships dock downtown, in Castries. Yachties ignore those peasants, who are of course richer by far than we are. None of the above have our advantage of socializing with the locals. They wouldn't know a bo'jou or a bo'swe if it came up and bit them.

Th other day we completed our activities after swimming class by taking five young tired hungry kids down to the river (actually a storm drain) to find guppies (who knows what they really were) to replace some that died after being fed apples. Much yelling, crying, dog-barking, and fighting ensued. All very predictable, for retirees. When the list of Great Ideas of the 21st Century is compiled, the Guppy Search of 2005 will not be among them. But remember, retirees must observe a basic grandparent rule: Do not say I Told You So. Your kids already know that.

The Retiree—March, 2005—St. Lucia

St. Lucia, West Indies:

Most people come to St. Lucia on ships. They sleep in air-conditioned cabins and take a tour of the market or the fort or the drive-in volcano. They see someone carrying a basket on her head. They buy a coconut bird feeder. They have a Piton beer or a Bounty rum punch. Then they leave for Martinique or Antigua.

We stay in a house with windows that are never closed, where the water supply has to be checked to see if it's still working, where our grandchildren live. We stay in Rodney Heights, where the houses don't have numbers and neither do the streets.

Rodney Heights has many dogs. Almost every house has a fence, and almost every fence has a dog or two. Or three. Air conditioners and fences are sold with a bonus dog to go with them.

Lucian dogs sleep all day and bark all night. Barking begins at midnight and stops just before sunrise. This barking routine is a Caribbean tradition of long standing.

Some barkers are independent contractors, roaming the streets looking for bark events, although dogs in fences are often self-initiating barkers needing little encouragement.

Barking follows a predictable pattern. A bark event, real or imagined, starts with a staccato bark burst. The call is picked up by a second barker, and then a third, fourth, fifth, etc. No single dog continues more than five minutes before stopping to listen. The listening break is about ten seconds. If no other bark is heard, a cease option is available, although seldom taken. If another bark is heard, no matter how distant, barking must continue.

Bark events include a door slamming on Martinique, about 30 miles away across the sea. Shutting of eyelids is another bark event, as is a mooing cow (yes there are cows wandering the streets), or a cat stomping its feet.

Sustained barking sessions continue for about an hour. At that point, dogs stop for a drink and gather in a discussion group. Performance is evaluated, usually vocally, after which routine barking resumes, usually triggered by the snapping shut of someone's eyelids.

Instigators are often soprano barkers. There are bass barkers and tenor barkers. Last night I heard a mezzo-soprano howler.

Minnesota barkers are dealt with by telephone, to the owners, not the barkers. One five-minute barking session triggers retribution. In St. Lucia, those who complain are told that dogs bark, and if you don't like it, maybe you should move.

We've grown accustomed to barking now. When we get home, we plan to get one of those barking-dog recordings—you know, Jingle Bells by yapping dogs—and play it all night. After all, a guy's got to get his sleep.

The Retiree—April, 2005—Trip

"So where ya been, anyway? Ain't seen ya around." Nels bumped into me at the grocery.

"Saint Lucia. Island."

"I like them ilands, so, Apossles? Up there on Superior? Musta been colt, ya? Do any fishin? Walleyes? Lakers? Maybe perch? Ice on them bays I spose, but not on da big lake. I like them trips. Coupla six-packs, meal worms, power auger, pick-em-up with a heater in back..."

"Not a cold island. Warm one. Caribbean. South of Martinique. Close to South America. Fly there. Sun and sand. Some fish, too, but we didn't catch any. Cast from shore. Mostly visited family. No heaters. No pick-em-ups except those little Japanese and Korean ones. Beers are small, maybe ten ounces. Small place, bad roads. Fourteen by twenty-seven miles, across the biggest part. Ground's too hard to dig worms, volcanic rock."

Nels looked curious. "Sister-in-law's been to Saint LuSeea. She got bit up and sunburned. That the same place? I been on lakes bigger'n that. Didn't catch any fish? Why go there? Dontcha eat fish?"

"Had flying fish, in a pot with the tail stuck in its mouth. Had baked fish, and fish soup. Kids caught little fish-bowl fish. Ate lots of chicken but not the good parts. Beef's not very good, and costs a lot."

"Fish soup? Flying fish? Beef's no good? Bad chicken? Ten-ounce beers? What the heck did ya go there for? Who needs that?" I don't think Nels would be a good traveling companion.

"Met a lot of nice people from all over the world," I offered. "Ecuador, India, Wales, England, Canada, Africa, Cuba, Japan. Lots of people go there to work for phone company, roads, resorts. Big resorts that'll give you anything you want for a price."

"Resorts here are good. Annandale's got some with great cottages. Walleyes, northerns, bass. Twelve-ounce beers, too. Price ain't bad, neither, if ya bring yer own boat."

"Scenery's best in the world," I countered. "Mountains go straight up from the sea. Breakers on the Atlantic. Sails on the Caribbean. Eighty-five degrees every day—that's thirty celsius. No snow boots, no jackets, no mittens."

"Shoot, we had thirty degrees here most of the time you was gone. And mountains ain't no big deal. Plenty waves in the summer, and I can wait for that. Beaches, too. Nice one by the highway there. Meet Canadians here, too, and Koreans, and Vietnamese, and there's some Pakistanis in Buffalo, I think. Mexicans instead of Cubans. Don't cost nothin to go here, I'm already here. Seems to me you just wasted a lotta money runnin' around for no good. No fish, bad roads, small beers, can't wear your Harley jacket, gotta fly there. You better think about trips like that. Coulda bought a power auger for what I'd have ta pay for one ticket, I betcha."

Maybe Nels is right. Life would be simpler if we confined our trips to Buffalo and Annandale. Still, once in awhile, it's nice to head out to someplace different. Someplace foreign. Like, maybe, Hutch or Alex.

The Retiree—April, 2005—Cleaning

I cleaned the basement. Oh, I'm sure if someone looked into the basement, they would tell me that I should clean the basement, but I did clean the basement. Cleaning the basement is a subjective thing, and clean to me is not the same as clean to some urban person without even a view of a lake. Or some non-retiree who hires things done.

All the Asian beetle shells were swept up and thrown out, although they looked good as new. Three single left-hand gloves are now in the garbage. It takes a lot of courage for me to throw out things. I found fuses that fit the main switch on a fuse box that has been gone since 1996. Accompanying them were some 20-amp fuses in their original carton, and an automobile fuse of the kind not seen since the seventies. I couldn't throw out perfectly good fuses, so they went into the cardboard box marked 'electrical,' along with forty switch plates and covers, ranging from molded porcelain to a pushbutton wall switch. They're all good as new, although some of them are fifty years old. Can't throw them.

The coffee can marked 'plumbing' now includes a wad of copper screws for holding down toilets. There must be fifty dollars worth of copper and brass in there. It will take two people to move the can. It's been painted to the workbench for nine years.

I found about 500 board feet of shims. I can never find a shim when I need one, which is every time I build or fix anything wooden, so I buy another pack. I am set for life with shims, but already I can't remember where I put them.

All the dog stuff is in one place now. She's got four combs, two brushes, a curry comb which come to think of it is hanging from the arbor outside, pills for problems she never had, soap for fleas she never had, and a can of flowery stuff that would make her kill me if I ever chanced to spray it on her. It will all be accessible in the remote chance that any of it is needed.

Gone now are many tools from the past. These are not tools anyone could use. They may have been good for opening cans or soldering pipe or tapping holes or timing 1933 Chevrolets or scraping paint. All were more or less useable, but since they hadn't found a use since 1951, out they went. I mourn their loss.

I built a shelf to hold the various oils I found. I have graphite for locks, spray for guns, pump cans full of 10W-30, petroleum jelly in a capless tube, graphite sticks for car locks (probably that '33 Chev), spray teflon, and unmarked stuff that certainly smells like oil. Could be band-aids or oakum or maybe a shop manual for a long-gone small engine; hard to tell, as it had soaked in some sort of slime for decades. Now it's right where I can find it.

One of these days I will take on the three or four tackle boxes down by the steps. Assuming I can get them open, I will rewind the drop lines, put hooks in plastic boxes, scrape the rust off the baits, separate the spoons, and salvage the pork rind. Maybe I can use that unmarked oil on my new shelf. It could come in handy for opening the folding knives.

The Retiree—April, 2005—Advice

With my vast experience at retiring, it's imperative that I help those of you who are working. Help you to figure out when to retire, that is, not how to work. I never did figure out how to work. But I retired five times.

Signals appear that tell one when it's time to retire. The signal may be simple; such as "Clean out your desk, and as soon as you log off the computer, your passwords will be revoked." I had that happen once, initiating my first retirement. I had lots of company then. Those outside the business, when I hinted at the rumors of a layoff, advised me that I just might be retiring. I didn't believe it because I had something else lined up. Rumors had been flying for months.

Signals may be obscure. You look around in a meeting and finds out that you are the oldest one there. By decades. Some of the attendees defer to you for answers, calling you "Mr. (activity)," where "activity" is whatever your company's business was. For example, "Tell us how it was done in the seventies, Mr. (or Ms.) Analyst," or "Explain how those buggy whips were braided, Mr. Teamster." Or they may just call you "Pops." In some cases, they won't talk to you at all. Take careful note when these cases arise.

Sometimes the boss drops little hints during reviews or casual conversation. "We have some really good candidates coming up, and it would be nice if they could see a career path opening up," he'll say.

"How's fishing up there at the lake place?" Ignoring those hints could put you in the situation I found in my third retirement.

The medical community can assist you in deciding when to retire. A little hint may be dropped by your doctor, when he says, "The tests were positive, and surgery should be as soon as possible. Have you eaten supper yet?" If you recover, you can rejoin the ranks of the employed later. Have the scar put in a place that can be covered by clothing, just in case.

Another signal can be given in a meeting, usually company-wide. The one in charge will say that things are about to change, such as "We've been bought out. Some of you will be contacted by the Texas office. All of you, hit the road now, before we release the dogs. Your severance checks are in the mail." On the way out, arrange regular meetings at a cheap restaurant. It helps to have people who will commiserate with you. Some don't call this retiring.

Bosses sometimes think they can lower the boom—oops, help your decision—without your noticing. They'll say, "You know, this business is a young person's game. I know you can handle the work. But you're looking a little tired. Are you feeling well? Hank, down on three, retired last year, and he's having the time of his life. And Bob, up on six, well you know how he keeled over at his desk. You sure you feel all right?" If you are able and strong, punch that sucker right in the beezer and walk.

A last hint: Arrange your pensions and medical coverage early. Don't tell anyone except those directly involved, such as the entire United States Government. Don't wait. Start now. If you are over age 35, it may be too late to get things done correctly. Believe me. I've been there.

The Retiree—Mayday, 2005—Trip

"Amish Raised Chickens," the sign said. All right, so what; the Amish raised chickens. But then maybe I was taking it wrong. Maybe they were selling raised chickens, something like raised doughnuts, but I don't know what a raised chicken is. Wife interrupted my ruminations with a comment that someone around that northern Illinois town was selling chickens that had been raised without any artificial chemical feed additives. I knew that must be wrong, because then the sign would have said "Amish-raised Chickens."

That's the sort of mind-broadening experience travel is. Yes, we traveled again. That's our job now that we're retired. We travel. According to my dictionary, the word travel is a variation of the word travail, which is an instrument of torture composed of three stakes. That's pretty close to right, when the goal is Chicago.

If you haven't gone to Chicago lately, next time you go you'll find that tolls on those confounded expressways have doubled. It cost me $3.40 in tolls to get to Candy's house, half way into that city, and we used to be able to go all the way through to Gary for something like $2.80. Not that we stopped in Gary on those trips; who would? I'm not counting the change that's now under the car seat, or the coins that fell out the window.

When I'm on I-290 I always think of things like flat tires or blown head gaskets or transmission failures. That didn't happen. If it had, I'd have abandoned the car, except that there's no place to walk. And everyone still drives 15 miles per hour over the limit. They even park fast. Save the toll increase by buying an automated toll sticker that gets read by a secret magic light. I accidentally drove through the secret magic light lane last time we were there, without a sticker. The ticket hasn't arrived in the mail yet. That part must be manual.

This trip was to celebrate the 90th birthday of a lovely aunt. Over 60 people wandered into cousin Candy's house that day. I knew about 12 of them, including my wife. There were loads of flowers and lots of pretty glass gifts and a big pile of cards and a tremendous mess of food and a cooler and a keg. We had a good time.

Another cousin said we could spend the night at her house, so we followed her through the outskirts of Chicago to her home. She has toned down her driving. Once before when we followed her, she drove 85 miles an hour and changed her planned route on the way. If we had missed a turn, we'd have ended up in Indiana, lost. She behaved well this time. We slept on a hide-a-bed shaped like this: WW. Friends or relatives always give us beds like that, as it makes us leave after one night. Having celebrated until 1 AM we slept well.

We look forward to family get-togethers, no matter whose family shows up. It's a welcome treat to talk to people you seldom see. Usually these get-togethers are funerals. This time the guest of honor was not lying down. We hope she continues that way for many more years.

The Retiree—May, 2005—Advice

"What do you want to do when you grow up?" I asked the kid.

"I want to be on Paid Administrative Leave," he replied. "That seems to me to be the best job around."

"Hmm. Maybe. But it wouldn't seem to give you much sense of accomplishment. Don't you want to get more out of your profession?"

"Yeah, sure. Sense of accomplishment. Like maybe a tax accountant. Or a dental assistant, with someone spitting on my hands," he grumbled. "Or how about a programmer, watching my job go to India. Or a phone operator, or a watchmaker. Or a prison guard. Or..."

"What are you? Maybe eight? Why don't you want to be a fireman or a doctor or a rock star, like all your friends?"

"Get real. Those dumb kids could never be doctors or firemen. No-talent boobs think they could go on stage. Give me Paid Administrative Leave any time. All the free time you want, no hassles, good pay. That's for me."

"How do you plan to get that enviable position?" I asked. "What will you study? How do you plan to become a Paid Administrative Leaver, or whatever you call it?"

"I've got my career path all laid out. Study is no problem. What's to study? I just plan to stay home. I like it at home," he smirked.

"Who would hire you? Someone has to put you on leave. Usually you go on Paid Administrative Leave because something went wrong.

You shot somebody. You're suspected in a theft. You were seen in a compromising situation. Something like that," I advised.

He was aghast. "Job? You mean I have to get a job first?" He lapsed into a profound depression. He mulled the situation over for some time, having had his dream shattered.

Then he brightened. He'd obviously come up with something that he considered on a par with his original objective. "Do you think congress will be able to get me a position in the First Tee Program in St. Augustine, Florida for a character education program? I found that on the web. It said the group's mission is to impact the lives of young people around the world by creating affordable and accessible golf facilities primarily to serve those who have not previously had exposure to the game and its positive values. They got a million bucks of your tax money to do that in 2004."

"Okay, I give up," I sighed. "Just run for public office, kid. You've got a future there."

The Retiree—May, 2005—Institutes

Since my invention of The Maple Lake Institute, devoted to practically nothing useful, I've been interested in how many other seemingly useless and maybe fraudulent institutes are out there. Being retired, I went Googling on the internet to investigate. I got 432,000,000 hits on the word 'Institute'. I read every one of them, of course, and found that they are (almost) all perfectly sincere. Here's a compendium of places to go (not all 432,000,000 are listed) in order to solve problems you possibly have, and a lot that you couldn't possibly have.

First, The Workplace Bullying and Trauma Institute, featured on a TV report recently (that's what set off my research). Then, Nice Guys' Institute, with research on getting girls (possibly as scientific as the Maple Lake Institute). Next, Institute on Finite Groups, by the Pure Mathematics Symposium (I go there a lot). The Buros Institute publishes the Mental Measurements Yearbook and Tests in Print (you can borrow my copy). Esalen Institute—forty-year-long Olympics of the body, mind, and spirit, committing themselves not so much to "stronger, faster, higher" as to deeper, richer, more enduring (how nice). Lucidity Institute—markets books and tapes on lucid dreams as well as lucidity induction devices. (What is a lucidity induction device? Something like a light bulb?)

Take a breath now. That's a lot to absorb. Here are more:

Asphalt Institute—international organization with information on Superpave (what?), environmental, technical questions, etc. The National Institute for Clinical Excellence—national clinical guidelines to secure consistent, high quality evidence (of something or other). Steel Recycling Institute—North American steel industry association that promotes and sustains the recycling of all steel products (such as my old Bronco). The Chile Pepper Institute of New Mexico State University—Educating the World About Chiles (a huge goal). Immortality Institute—conquer the blight (?) of involuntary death; a 501(c)(3) nonprofit educational (nice to know it's tax advantaged). Armenian National Institute—Affirmation of the 1915 Armenian Genocide committed by Ottoman Turkey, featuring photos, documents, maps, chronology, resolutions, bibliographies (I never knew). The Singularity Institute for Artificial Intelligence—a 501(c)(3) nonprofit (you can contribute) researching beneficial Artificial Intelligence (how about non-beneficial, or non-artificial?). Josephson Institute of Ethics—a nonpartisan, nonprofit organization working to improve the ethical quality of society by advocating principled (as opposed to unprincipled) reasoning . Danmarks Meteorologiske Institut—Vejrinformationer for Danmark og farvandene omkring Danmark (well, ya). Max-Planck-Institute betreiben Grundlagenforschung in den Natur-, Bio- und Geisteswissenschaften im Dienste der Allgemeinheit (I always liked Max). There's a Russian institute or two but my word processor doesn't support Russian alphabetic characters. Broad Institute—Public-private consortium to create comprehensive tools for uncovering the functions of human, mouse genes (Harvard, I think).

That should be the full circle of subjects, from Nice Guys' research on getting girls, to Broad Institute. There's a place I know that will let me set up a web site free. Maybe the Maple Lake Institute will be number 432,000,001 when someone else Googles Institute. It's a cinch I won't do it again.

The Retiree—May, 2005—Memorial Day

I got caught between wars. It wasn't my fault. When in places like Branson they ask if I'm a veteran, I hesitate. The National Guard let me go to meetings for around six years, and I spent half a year crawling around in the dirt of Missouri. I learned how to dig holes and blow up things, but for the most part, I only worried about being activated. My activation had to do with an oil spill on the Minnesota River, where we actually saw one dead duck, and ate in a pretty good restaurant. They also serve who only stand and wait, I guess. But it doesn't seem very significant.

We all know stories of our current activated reservists. It's not the same now as when I was in the Guard. People are blowing up people, not things, and jobs are being interrupted for long periods. We celebrate real warriors and owe some real debts again.

Sixty-three years ago or so, my childhood was disrupted by a world war. We played war games, dug foxholes in the empty lot, pretended to be heroes. We wondered why there was a poster in the grocery store that said "Loose Lips Sink Ships" when we'd never even seen a ship. Especially on Lyndale Avenue.

We had a world map tacked behind the door, where we tried to track various uncles. Dad was a little older than most draftees and had a critical defense job, so he was home, except for long hours of work. Jimmy's dad was home, too, with a reserve unit that stayed local.

Ronnie's dad was in another defense job, and was a little old for service, working those long hours, as did his mom.

Uncle Vern joined the Marines for a second time, and went to the South Pacific, where things were anything but pacific. Uncle Rol was a Marine out there, too, a cook. Uncle Dan was an Army carpenter, building in the Pacific. Uncle Clint helped maintain B-26s in Alaska. Uncle Berney served aboard a submarine tender in the Pacific. Uncle Bud was in the Merchant Marine, dodging German subs in the Atlantic.

Later, Cousin Danny got his helmet dented in Korea. Cousin Russ was also a Marine then. I was still too young to do anything but worry and pray.

On Memorial Day we celebrate those people. Once a year we look at and think about freedom and graveyards with rows of crosses and stars. Once a year it sinks in again, that freedom must be won and re-won. Where would we be without Patrick Henry, Nathan Hale, Sergeant York, Audie Murphy, Vern, Rol, Dan, Clint, Berney, Bud, Danny, Russ, and millions of others?

Most of the above are gone now. But there are plenty of current servicemen and women around. Thank them when you see them. And remember the rest.

The Retiree—June, 2005—Caveats

"It ain't my fault!" I cry, but nobody seems to notice. I'll get blamed for it whether or not it was my fault. But I've figured out what to do about it. I am constructing a caveat, taking my cues from the masters, the lawyers who put together corporate caveats for practically everything. You've heard the gibberish on the radio, you've seen the small print on your television screens, that say in effect we've got a big sale on but it's not for you, or this pill will cure you but if it hurts you it isn't our fault. It's your fault for buying the thing, you gullible dummy.

Here are real life examples. I've disguised the names of the companies since they'd sue me for being honest, and I can't afford to do anything irresponsible until I create my own caveat.

"Nondeposit investment products are not insured by the FDIC, are not deposits or other obligations of or guaranteed by [us], and involve investment risks, including possible loss of the principal...Past performance does not guarantee future results. We consider our sources reliable (why the caution, then?). Accuracy and completeness are not guaranteed. Information is subject to change. Transactional details should not be relied on for tax purposes...Messaging...is not intended for solicitation purposes (right). Electronic mail...is not secure. We will not accept time-sensitive, action-oriented messages, transaction orders, fund transfer instructions or check stop payments electronically. If you are not the intended recipient, notify the Sender.

This information is intended only for the person named above...Do not distribute...without written consent of the author. Non-business opinions may not reflect opinions of [us]. [We] reserve the right to monitor all e-mail."

That's what it says. What it means is, "You can't trust us. We may not know anything reliable, and we wouldn't tell you if we did. If you buy something we told you about, we didn't mean it. Don't come crying if somebody rips you off. We don't do taxes. Stuff you buy is your fault, and we get to keep the money."

Here's another: "This communication is for use by the intended recipient and contains information that may be privileged, confidential or copyrighted under applicable law. If you are not the intended recipient,...any use, copying or distribution of this e-mail, in whole or in part, is strictly prohibited. Please notify the sender by return e-mail and delete this e-mail...Unless explicitly and conspicuously designated as "E-Contract Intended", this e-mail does not constitute a contract offer, a contract amendment, or an acceptance of a contract offer. This e-mail does not constitute a consent to the use..." Yada yada yada.

What it means is "We don't know who sent this, but we didn't. If you think we will do what we say, you're mistaken and possibly nuts. Don't try to reply. We're leaving the office and we won't be back."

Henceforth, any correspondence from me will include the following: "Whatever I said, forget it. It's privileged information. I may deny it later, or maybe not; it's up to me. Anyway, it wasn't meant for you in the first place. If it's to my advantage, okay, otherwise too bad, you lose. Print the message, delete it from your e-mail, burn the copy, and eat the ashes." There. Now just try to corner me.

The Retiree—June, 2005—Fish

The weeds down by the lake were becoming a little overpowering, to the point that we had some difficulty finding the boat, so I decided to trim them. I like to keep the neighborhood neat. Hints from the neighbors (moving out, burning down their house) have sensitized me to the need to cut the weeds from time to time.

In the process of trimming, I felt someone watching me. It was a calm day, and when I looked at the water, I noticed five sunfish. They were all looking directly at me. Don't accuse me of an overactive imagination. I was standing close to the water and they were staring directly at me, all five of them.

Obviously, they were discussing me and the dog. In some cases, sunfish converse almost audibly. This fact is known only to a few of us. The dog and I are among those privileged few.

Reading fish lips isn't easy, but careful observation of the gills gives some clues as to the words being formed. Here's what appeared to be said by that group of five:

"There's that stupid dog again. She's the one who chewed on Sam that day when the little girl-kid dragged him up on the dock. If he'd been a little bigger, they'd have kept him and there'd be no more Sam," said a bluegill.

A pumpkinseed remarked, "The guy has a fly rod. Be careful of bugs when he's around. What's he doing now? He was facing the land instead of the lake. How do they breathe? I hate it when he chops weeds and they fall into the lake. Maybe if he drags the electric cord into the water…"

Another replied, "Don't get your hopes up. He's probably got a ground fault interruptor."

Well, you get the idea. Fish aren't usually too vocal, but they have a good deal more intelligence than one would suspect. The dog studied the water, seemed to understand the fish, but didn't see fit to tell me her observations. Usually, her concerns are with killing and eating things. She sees fish better from the dock, but from that vantage she can't read their lips. When she does talk, it's in growly tones and has something to do with hunger or thirst or entertainment, her only concerns since she got spayed, and I haven't been able to translate word for word yet.

I anticipated providing a great deal more information about animal communication in this column, but it thundered, and now I must go drag the dog out from under the steps to the garage. She's hiding from Thor, the Norse god of thunder, war, and strength, who she is certain will pound her into the ground with his hammer. Whenever she hears thunder, she does what every good guard dog does. She cowers in the dark like a sniveling coward. We've found her behind the toilet, in the shower, in the closet, in the basement, and under the bed during those stressful times. Today's foray into outside steps behind the formerly beautiful flowers is a new venture. If I don't get there quickly, my ordinarily understanding and loving spouse will likely send the dog to sleep with the fish.

Terrorized as she is, maybe she wouldn't care. After all, it's dark there, too.

The Retiree—June, 2005—Building

"How's the house plan coming? We've been waiting for the digging to start," I said to the owner of the empty lot next door.

"It's going fine," he said, optimistically. "Only one or two little catches. Somebody in authority thinks our house will be too big, and they think we need a toilet, and a septic tank will have to be buried fifty feet deep to fit in the hill, and people think our new house will not fit on the lot no matter what size we make it, and there are others who think we need to move the place a little south and east, and some want to saw down that tree up there, the only tree of its type remaining in the county, and probably the most beautiful tree of any kind in any county, and I just found someone who thinks your well is too close to my mound system, and if they don't get busy building, the wall down by the lake will wash out from the high water, and it looks like we will have to move the planned steps from the deck that won't be in the right place if we have to move the house plan, and we don't know if we can put in a driveway to the garage that may have to be made smaller, and I have to find a place to put my boat trailer and my little trailer and my bigger trailer and my kid's trailer, and when they dug in this ugly fence for construction they ruined what should be left of my lawn. And I just got bit by a mosquito. Otherwise, it's going fine."

"Good. I like the plan, too. I like it more than the Department of Natural Resources, who came out to check what you're doing to preserve the Spotted Elkworm and the Pileated Wiggleweed in the lake. They don't like your roller, you know. And the ragweed is getting out of hand." I like to encourage people. It's just the way I am.

"Nobody called me about worms and weeds," he said, frowning.

"Maybe it was in that letter they tried to deliver the other day. The mailperson said something like hey, they don't have a mailbox, and my wife said, hey, they don't have a house either, so she said could we deliver it, and we of course said yes, but I can't for the life of me remember where we put it. Oh, well, it was probably an ad," I said.

"We gave them our address. Both of them," he mulled, thoughtfully. "I'll call them, whoever they were. I have to call everybody in the government, anyway. And I have to see the plumber, electrician, well driller, septic, grading..." His voice weakened. "Paving, cement work, architect, county, DNR..." He sighed. "Windows, doors, garage door, lighting, tile, carpet, surveyer, dock, stone work..." Blood was seeping from his ears. "Painter, permits, drywall, flooring..." He began to shout. "Where will it end? What can I do? Wiggleweeds, elkworms, ragweed!"

"A new house, though. It'll be worth it," I encouraged.

"What new house?" he screamed. "I've got a house already! And I'm going to it right now!"

I suppose he'll be back next weekend. Meanwhile, I'll cut some ragweed. It's the least I can do.

The Retiree—July, 2005—Mildew

Apologies to those who are suffering from the raised level of Maple Lake. And to those whose land may have sunk a little because of the drop in the water table. I had to clean my pontoon boat, and there was mildew on it. Mold, mildew, moss, maybe a few weeds, and a couple very small trees.

Where all that mildew came from I can't imagine. The boat was kept in a barn last winter, and I'm willing to bet that none of the cows was mildewed. But there it was, green and black, and getting thicker by the minute.

I decided to research how to get rid of mildew. Webster tosses around words to describe it such as smut, fungus, rust, decay, spoil. When I looked it up in the Bible, the definitive authority on how to clean up things, I found this in Deuteronomy: "...with a consumption...fever...inflammation...extreme burning...sword...blasting...mildew..." It certainly looked serious.

I was up against it. I didn't have a sword or (hardly) any explosives, so I hooked up all the hoses I possess and used my highest powered nozzle. The "extreme burning" turned out to be sunburn, and it wasn't too bad, as there were some clouds. Everything was too wet to use explosives. A brush, a broom, a screwdriver, soap, a compound called oxy-something (oxymoron, oxygenated, oxidant, or oxheart—my eyes were a little blurry from fumes) seemed to do better than just plain muscle, a diminishing resource anyway. As a result of my chemicals, my feet became a little cleaner than they had been.

Mildew is persistent. Carpeting and maybe tires should be made of pure mildew. Blasting it with the nozzle tended to weld it to my paddleboat, to my legs, and to the inside of my eyelids.

After a few hours of work, I rolled up the hose and went in for lunch. My peanut butter tasted like mildew, and the glass of milk was a little green. There are now dark blotches on the dock, something slippery on the grass, spots on the car (in the garage with the door shut), and a green loon floating out in the middle of the lake.

Recovery from the mildew issue took a few days, during which I had a birthday and after which I attacked weeds on my boat's pontoons. The weeds, delicate, flowing, like a grass skirt, waving gently in the current, slowed the boat and had to be removed. My Caribbean daughter had given me just the tool—a cutlass. Up here we call them machetes. Mine is a little like a medieval battle-ax, only a bit more lethal-looking. In St. Lucia, they are used to chop down trees, harvest bananas, trim grass, dig holes, wave at friends, intimidate enemies, build piers, mend boats, shave, cut meat, and, of course, take weeds off pontoons. It worked marvelously.

That's the last time I try to go against nature. Mildew is obviously part of some grand plan, and removing it can only result in an imbalance. Life itself may be threatened. From now on, you'll see me riding around in a green pontoon boat with a grass skirt. The boat, that is.

The Retiree—July, 2005—Sizes

Supermarkets are laid out all wrong. Not that I'm any kind of expert on layout. I've done a lot of it, but mostly computer print layouts and pictures on walls and kitchen floors and stuff like that. But I am a consumer, and as a retiree I am opinionated, and that's enough expertise for anyone.

We were shopping in one of those megastores when Wife said "Go get some toothpicks." There is never a Toothpick Aisle; I know that. There may be a Picnic Aisle, or a Paper Goods Aisle, or a Baking Aisle, or a Miscellaneous Aisle with things like motor oil and ant poison, but there is no Toothpick Aisle. So I went on an unguided search, looking through the frozen foods and the canned vegetables and the bread. The toothpicks were in the Frozen Food Aisle, near the kites or scoops or some other unrelated stuff, hanging on some sort of bracket that didn't belong there.

That's when I realized that supermarkets are laid out all wrong. And that I personally hold the key to sanity in the layout business.

Stuff needs to be in categories by size and shape. Never mind what the stuff is. Especially in superstores, where you can buy fishing licenses and steam tables and vanilla and sewing needles and lawn tractors, things need to be sorted by size and shape.

There should be a Big Round Aisle, where you buy round things like bowling balls, watermelons, gas cans, paper towels (sets of four), toilet paper (bunches of twelve), bags of ice, or hub caps (four). I know paper towels and TP aren't round but in my mind they fit the category, and these are my rules, so that's how it should be.

There should be a Little Aisle, with toothpicks, spices, fish hooks, needles, radishes, pens, ant poison, and jewelry. You can think of a bunch of other little things. Pepper, fish food, vitamins, things like that.

A Big Square Aisle would be for things with corners, like floor tile, lasagna, trailers, and some meats for large families. Put encyclopedias there. And large cereal boxes.

There should be a One-Hand Aisle. Lots of things are one-handable. It would include cans and small packaged goods, such as CDs, boxes of 6 candy bars, fishing lures, and books. Corn, motor oil, beer, small foam footballs, toy cars, The Reader's Digest, and other things that can be grabbed with one hand, even if you have a sore shoulder, should all be put in one place.

Smelly Aisle could be a sort of exception to the shape rule. Included there would be plant food, some drugs, plastic toys, spices, hot sauce, smoked meats, and foot powder (a little stretch of the imagination for that one).

By now you're pretty tired of the whole idea. But just think: Wife says get some toothpicks, or get some stickees, or get birthday candles, and zoom, there you go to the Little Aisle. No more wandering around, trying to determine what some food manager was thinking when he hid the product on the top shelf. And, just maybe, on the way, you'll find a new bass bait.

The Retiree—July, 2005—Building

Fifty years ago I was a cement finisher's helper for the biggest contractor in Minneapolis—he must have weighed 350 pounds. His crew was only maybe 15 people.

Among those people on the crew were Axel, a grumpy old Swede, and Maynard, the most profane man in the world at the time. Those two people directed most of my cement finishing help. Maynard usually complained about the blocks he was given, and Axel would spit his snoose into the driveways he was finishing. They both advised me as to the quality of the work I did. Loudly.

I learned a lot from those two. I learned that I didn't want to push wheelbarrows full of concrete and carry blocks for a living, and I learned a lot of new words that I'd rather not use.

Lately, the neighbors have had a crew of blocklayers and cement finishers out to start construction on their new home. The trade has changed. Nobody uses a wheelbarrow. Now they use a truck with a conveyor on it. The driver uses a wireless remote to direct the conveyor to anyplace his happy little heart desires. The cement finishers and their smooth-muscled helpers push the stuff around with gloved hands. Once the driver actually shook hands with the cement finisher, who took off his glove to do the shaking. A glove! A handshake! Axel would have been aghast. I talked to one of the truck drivers. He spoke of his broker, and his portfolio. Maynard thought a portfolio was a musical instrument.

Building on lakeshore can be a problem. There's a hill. There has to be, or the lake would be all over the lot. The neighbor is going to need some fill to make a house level on a hill like that. I figure he'll need about the same amount of fill that it would take to cover South Carolina to a depth of two feet. The lake side of the house, on completion, will be perhaps fifty feet above my roof, and the road side of the house will be underground.

Fortunately I am around to guide and advise the contractors and the neighbor. I give the neighbor regular updates via e-mail. Sometimes he shows up quickly after my updates. I sent him a picture of the Pyramid at Cheops (I couldn't find a good picture of the Great Wall of China) and told him it was his basement wall, but I don't think he bought that one, or he was in shock, as it took a day for him to come out.

A trailer just showed up with a bunch of 6x6 timbers on it. Either someone has decided to change the house design to one of those half-timbered European buildings, or the concrete business ran out of materials and is sending a substitute. It's obvious that they are going to need my supervision. Additionally, there are lots of new places for me to scratch my initials.

It's a good thing I'm retired, and am constantly around to help. Maybe I can show those kids some wheelbarrow techniques. I know they'll appreciate it.

The Retiree—August, 2005—War

During WWII, when my main concern was getting across Lyndale Avenue on my way to McKinley grade school, a friend, let's call her "V" for now, was crawling under German train cars to keep from being strafed by British and American attackers. While I was watching Clarence throw wads of library paste at the ceiling and spending time sitting in the corner for doing so, V was watching the Royal Air Force's elite Bomber Group No. 5 drop incendiary bombs on Würzburg.

V is strong, capable, sure of herself, not afraid to tell you how she feels about things. Widowed now, she lives with two cats in a quiet, pleasant American townhouse, wildlife at her window, the city out her door.

I am learning about V's past, to make a record of those days long ago for her son. She says she can't write, hasn't any talent, needs someone to provide a little aid. With all the things she's done, I really think she'd do a great job of writing, too, but I'm privileged to help.

A glimpse at the documents V is using to refresh her memory provides insight. Her mother typed up memories of their journey to relative safety. The notes are typed in German, inserted into an old diary, and look fragile after all those years. V said the diary is private and can't be disturbed. It was her mother's property, not hers. But the notes are separate, and can be used.

Her mother was about thirty when she took her daughter and fled

Poland, after her father was reported missing in action. Since he'd served in the Latvian army, he was certain he'd not be called to duty, but he found himself conscripted into the German army. He most likely was captured in Romania by the Russians, as a spy. Spies were shot.

My contributions to V's story are limited. I've looked up history as presented in the websites of places such as Würzburg, Poznan, and Schweinfurt, and have been impressed by the way the various histories are written. For example, Würzburg's website gives the following thoughts about the war, after discussing a firebombing that killed about 5,000 people:

> *"May their terrible fate serve as a solemn warning and reminder to us of our duty to remain aware that in our daily lives every hurtful word, every form of disrespectful behaviour towards our fellow human beings might, if it is not halted, lead to other far more devastating forms of hatred and violence. We must remember that it is the duty of each and every one of us to build and maintain a peaceful world."*

There are no comments about vicious Brits, vengeful Americans. There are comments about 20 million Russians who died, 6 million who died in concentration camps, and the many others who suffered, such as V.

Sorry for my abandoning the carefree tone I usually take in this space. I've been overtaken by recollections of someone who was there, who saw the bombs, who ran from machine guns, who went hungry, whose family was torn apart. Maybe I'll give you a few more peeks into the past, later. Right now, I need to take a walk.

The Retiree—August, 2005—Syndromes

My computer dictionary tells me that a syndrome is a number of symptoms occurring together and characterizing a specific disease or condition or any set of characteristics regarded as identifying a certain type, condition, etc.

My antique collegiate dictionary says it's a group of signs and symptoms that occur together and characterize a disease.

Google tells me that there are lots of syndromes such as Asperger, Marfan, Sjogren's, Carpal Tunnel, Chronic Fatigue, Restless Leg, Geek (I didn't look that one up), Noonan, and about 24,100,000 others that it found out there in the ether someplace. (I gotta quit using Google. Maybe I have Google Syndrome. Or Geek Syndrome.)

In case I appear insensitive, I apologize to those who have a significant syndrome. But I think the word is a cop-out and represents the tendency to hedge your bets. The doctor or analyst or practitioner who says you have a syndrome is telling you he's not sure if you have Restless Leg syndrome or if you had too much coffee, so you might as well take this pill for $85 a month for the rest of your life, which may not be too long if the cautions on the label are right. Now I have to apologize to the entire medical community, too.

Back in antiquity, when my collegiate dictionary was new, nobody had a syndrome. They had a disease. It was for sure. You didn't have Chronic Fatigue syndrome; you had rheumatism or the ague or vile humours of the night air or demon possession or a test tomorrow, and that was definite. Get some exercise, take two aspirins and call me in the morning, shape up you lazy twit.

Either get rid of the "syndrome" syndrome, or call a lot of other things syndromes. Maybe then we will get back to defined problems and call a spade syndrome a spade syndrome.

My boat had a battery syndrome when we launched it this spring. The ash tree has an electric line syndrome and needs trimming. The dog has a shedding syndrome. My front tooth had a chip syndrome but the dentist applied a syndromatic hole filler with some sort of magic syndrome curing light.

Just by overusing the word, I think it will fall into disuse. For example, who hears anything about airdromes any more? Back in the 'thirties, there were lots of them. We didn't need airdromes and we don't need syndromes.

Here's my suggestion for everyone: Call anything you please a syndrome. I have a thirst syndrome, so get me some coffee, and a hunger syndrome, make it a hamburger, and if you hurry it up I'll give you a big tip syndrome. Send me that clothing syndrome on page 57 of your catalog, item 3, and I'll pay with my credit card syndrome. Give me the starting syndrome so I can start the car. By calling everything a syndrome, we will suffer greatly for a little while, but after everyone is sick of syndromes, the world will be a better place.

Don't thank me. It's a public service syndrome.

The Retiree—August, 2005—Riff-raff

"Timmy and Tammy have a time-share? I never heard about that," I said.

"In Florida," she said. "Not far from Yalaha. Away from the riff-raff."

"Tim and Tam? Time share? Yalaha? Away from riff-raff? One of those where they can exchange weeks?"

"Maybe. Tim and Tam could go to Walla Walla. Or Flin Flon." She was getting into it now.

"Ogallala would be a nice stop on the way to Vegas. TimTamOgallala." Two can play that game.

"Vegas advertises hanky-panky. They're too old for hanky-panky. They should stick to Tallahassee if they don't go to Yalaha. Nicer than Flin Flon or Walla Walla, and still no riff-raff. Not like Tuba City," she opined.

Well, I can take up the cudgel with the best of them; at least with the best of them what has a couple thesauruses—thesauri?—on his computer. I can click with the best of them which clicks. I tossed out, "Are those time-shares ticky-tacky?" in the vain hope that I'd get ahead while bringing up a thesaurus on the screen. "Do they wear flip-flops there, or are they wishy-washy?"

She turned away to hide her amusement. Now, she says it was to hide her disgust, but I'm sure it was to hide her amusement. "There's always Lackawanna," she tossed off, generating palpable brain waves while she rubbed her forehead.

The world was my oyster, whatever the heck that means. "Personally, I'd try for Australia. Burrumbeet or Buninyong. Sturt Street in Ballarat may have a Chi-Chi's. Moonambel or Dalwhinnie are a little too hot for a time share. And they have riff-raff." Take that.

She drew herself up to her full height, or maybe a little less, because of that stiff back of hers. "You twit. If you want to remain my dou-dou, just find a place like Piti Pito', put on your flip-flops and shut up yo' bus' about Sturt Street. I'm done with riff-raff, Yalaha, flip-flops, ticky-tacky, Walla Walla, Ogallala, Flin Flon, wishy-washy, Tuba City, hanky-panky, Moonabel, and Lackawanna. I'm going to make supper."

"What are we having, my dove?" I queried, quietly.

"Boiled bologna, brown beans, baked bread, big bagels, boxed biscuits, brown betty, black..."

"STOP," I cried. "I give up. Wait, I don't quite give up. It's just that food thing. Not only don't I know anything about food, but you're making me hungry. Let's take a break. Maybe we can give Tim and Tam a call. Ask about Flin... Oh, never mind. It can wait."

The Retiree—September, 2005—Water

Well, the feared event happened. It took lots of rain to make it start, but it happened more or less as we anticipated. "It" was the collapse of the neighbor's place.

Not to mislead anyone, their brand new house-a-building didn't collapse. The lot did.

Earlier I may have mentioned the enormous lot of fill required to permit ordinary humans to enter the lake side of their new house. The neighbor may have perceived that viewpoint in my several e-mails to him regarding that movement of dirt, not quite equal to that displaced in building the Panama Canal. The dirt stayed where it should have, until a big truck and trailer brought a load of drywall. It got stuck somewhere near where the Gatun Locks would later appear. Another equally large truck came to pull it out. The two trucks dug a trench deeper than the Minnesota Valley near New Ulm. Unfortunately, the trench was dug the day before the Great September Deluge, when we got half a foot of hard rain.

About 10:30 p.m. that night, when I was re-routing a newly created river in my swimming suit, I realized that I'd come into possession of a great quantity of clean fill, and it was headed for my canoe. Seeing the futility of the river dredging project, I retreated to my basement which was rapidly filling with water and frogs. To Wife and I it looked hopeless. Bewildered and tired, we did the logical thing. We opened the overhead door, dried off, and went to bed.

The next day, our lot looked a lot more like his lot than a lot of lots do, and his lot showed a lot more house than he wanted to see. The canoe was safe, but it had caused a great eddy in the new river's current, and the resulting sand bar can be seen from space.

The normally affable crew of builders showed up in the morning with shovels. To their credit and my delight, they attacked our lot with lots of zeal and vigor, putting the lot back where it belonged, and revealing a lot of really tired grass. It was a lot of effort. They shoveled heroically almost all day long. They found our picnic table and patio, but the flowers were for the most part gone. Lots of them may have disappeared regardless, with rain of that significance.

Some of the flowers may be in our tuck-under boathouse/basement, which accumulates lots of water whenever we get half a foot of rain, when the rock-sump floor drain turns into a spring, and water cascades merrily around the house and down in front of the overhead door. The frogs of the night before had gone to seek refuge someplace a little drier.

All's well that ends well, though. The neighbors are buying lots of rock to reinforce the lot, and a bobcat restored something approaching a normal grade around their house. We found some bags of donated grass seed by our door. Part of the Canoe Peninsula has been restored to the lakeshore. The basement is once again dry.

The builders haven't been seen, though. Has anyone observed lots of contractor trucks outside of the chiropractor's office?

The Retiree—September, 2005—Sculpture

Construction of the neighbor's house proceeds apace. Big trucks show up regularly, and they seem to know what to do, and when to do it, with one or two exceptions, come to think of it, involving towing one another out of the holes they made.

The latest work has to do with concrete. I did some concrete work half a century ago. Concrete hasn't changed since then. People still wear rubber boots and carry long sticks with flat boards on the end of them and appear to be very serious about where the stuff goes and doesn't go because if it goes in the wrong place, it becomes a part of the world that never changes, a little like Palisade Head or Easter Island or Ayer's Rock.

I figured there must be some concrete left over after they finished pouring the various floors, so I asked if I could have a stack or a bundle or a dishful or whatever would be appropriate. The lump they provided was sufficient to create a sculpture, my intention in the first place.

Michelangelo's "David" was what came to mind. Should be easy, I thought, as it's already been done once. With little hesitation, I began my quest for lasting beauty, for personal glory, for something to endear myself to the neighbors and their children and their children's children to time immemorial.

"David" turned out to be very challenging. I didn't know what kind of sling he had. More appropriate would be King Leopold of Belgium or

St. Patrick, to celebrate the neighbors' heritage. I figured there'd be less of a chance of someone knowing what St. Patrick looked like than the King, so I chose him. I immediately commenced my most serious attempt at sculpture since I made the clay head of classmate Harris back in high school. Harris disappeared immediately after graduation but I don't think the sculpture had anything to do with that. Someone said he's in Maine. Hiding.

St. Patrick would appear at the top of the driveway, pointing the way to the neighbor's house with a dead snake, in my artistic vision. It would be backlit at night, with a spotlight on the snake, visible to all from about a furlong away, where the road makes a turn. There would be reflectors set in his eyes, and the house number on his knees, two digits on each. I found the reflectors on two bicycles hanging from my garage rafters; not too big a sacrifice to make for neighbors.

The project went fairly well, considering. My wife compared it to a sawhorse I made many years ago out of scrap lumber. That worked, although I got negative comments about it from just about anyone who saw it, especially the wife, who called it a horse saw most of the time. I never found out why. It was destroyed in the Great Move South, ending my second retirement. But I digress.

Wet concrete has a tendency to get a little limp without proper support. I knew that. But I figured St. Patrick would have gotten a little tired later in life from chasing snakes, and with all those potatoes in his diet, he may have become, well, portly. But I must admit that it really didn't come out well.

Does anyone need a fairly respectable statue of Jabba the Hut?

The Retiree—October, 2005—Water

During the latest monsoon, we were wondering where the dog was. She hadn't been seen since the first thunder sounded over Dassel or someplace. She could hear it, but of course we couldn't for another hour or so.

There she was, behind the toilet. She stayed there for two days until she finally climbed into the bathtub. Now she's in the closet. We are eagerly awaiting sunshine so her bladder will not crystallize. We don't think she can wait more than four days before she pops.

The yard is covered with dirt again, from the neighbor's construction. The dock is under water but I think we can still locate it with an oar. Fuzzy oak galls or something cover our driveway and lawn. The oil in the lawnmower needs changing but I can't find the lawn and the air filter is full of fuzz anyway. The road looks like a sponge, and I can't afford to start the 4WD, so we're trapped. As soon as the rain stops, I will go try to read the rain gauge, if it hasn't run over or washed away. We're almost out of bread, and I need a haircut, and there are holes in my rain boots, both of them. It's dark and the electric bill just came so I don't want to turn on the lights. Someone put the shovel out in the rain, probably me, and it doesn't float, but I think I can find it with that oar. A pontoon boat floated by with the cover on, and nobody on it, but I just let it go because I was in a funk, but I did tie up three boats when they broke loose, and only one of them was mine. Dead weeds have built up on the lakeshore to a depth of fourteen feet, but they seem to be stopping the erosion. There's water in the basement again, but it hasn't reached the furnace; when it does, the house will probably explode. Nobody sends me e-mails except some guy who wants me to buy stock and people who want me to call my senators. Some nervous person keeps tearing the top off my mouse pads, and the mouse is collecting dog fur. Bali keeps getting bombed but I can't afford to run away there, anyhow. The paddleboat is floating again, and I pulled it up ten feet on shore before all this rain. The canoe is probably still safe, though, if I could see it through the fog and rain. The garbage is starting to smell, but I don't want to go out any more than the dog does. Wind is blowing the thermometer off the tree.

Wait. It looks like there's a break in the clouds. And if I look closely at the dirt covering the lawn, I think I can see the shovel handle. Maybe there's some hope. Maybe if I work fast, before the freeze, I can excavate the back door and drain the basement. Hope springs eternal. If only spring would spring eternal…

The Retiree—October, 2005—Vermin

The mice are coming, the mice are coming!

Twice a year, spring and fall, mice decide that living outside stinks, and they need to find someplace warm where they can snuggle down and maybe do a little reading and pass away the cold winter.

Our dog informs us that there are suspicious creatures around, such as the Schwan's man or skunks or mice, but she does precious little to exterminate any of them. She will sniff around the cold air chute or make funny noises by the basement door or look around the fireplace, but nothing ever comes of it. Outside, we hear an owl at night and see the county eagle fly by but nobody stops for lunch. Dispatching the little intruders seems to be up to me. (Not the Schwan's man; we invited him.)

Our basement is a little unusual. Since it is forty years old in the new part and over fifty in the old crawl space, mice have no trouble finding spots where they can gain ingress, and in the fall when we do a lot of cleanup, the basement overhead door is often open anyway. A buffalo could come in from time to time.

Wife found an acorn under the sink the other day, reminding me that chipmunks once used the walls for storage when the place was a cabin. Apparently one of them returned to check out his former digs. How he got in is a mystery, unless he followed a buffalo.

Traps are the answer. At least, that's the current approach. The critters have definite places to go and routes to take in order to bed down or find a good reading light or locate bugs or sandwiches or whatever they want to eat. I think I know most of those routes, and that's where the traps go. Poison works, too, but there's usually no evidence that anything happened, except for empty boxes. I need physical evidence. I need a corpse.

Recently I caught a vole. This one had a really pretty black coat. If they were maybe fifty pounds, they'd be sought after for their fur. As it is, they are relegated to my fire pit. By the way, in the process of incineration, they smell terrible.

I'd really appreciate a little advice. If anyone knows how to convince the mouse population in general how important it is to avoid coming into the house, I'm listening. Don't suggest a cat. Our daughter's dog, who lives here now for at least a few more years, hates cats and will devour anything that looks even remotely feline, probably including skunks.

My idea of the perfect vermin would be a big vole that comes in from time to time to eat those icky Asian beetles, and then creeps out silently without rousing the dog, sealing up its hole when it leaves, and arranging itself on the driveway to be collected for its fur when it perishes. Let me know if you find one of those.

The Retiree—October, 2005—Progress

There were no twist ties when I was a kid. I don't think anything was used to hold the end of bread wrappers together. Wrappers were waxed paper, not plastic, so they had a sort of natural adhesive that kept them together. One piece. No ties.

Milk bottles had little paper caps that had a tab with a tiny staple to keep it from tearing. Now we have bulky plastic things to recycle. Those old bottles were brought back to the store, in my case Grandpa's store, a couple blocks away. There was nothing but that little cap to throw away. Grandpa carried Franklin milk, brought by Sammy the milkman. Sammy was upset when they took away his horse and made him use a truck, because the truck wouldn't follow him down the alley, but that was before my time. Alleys are disappearing. Trucks made his work harder.

Grandma had rubber bands wrapped around her closet doorknob. She was a saver. I don't think she ever used any of the bands, we called them binders, but she couldn't bear to throw one away. The house was torn down for the freeway about 25 years ago, and I bet the rubber bands were still on the doorknob.

When I rolled up the toothpaste tube back then it stayed rolled, not like those annoying plastic tubes that try to assume their original shape regardless of the quantity of paste. Toothpaste tubes are supposed to stay rolled up. What happened? You call that progress?

Uncle Bud bought the first television set in the extended family. It was a round ten-inch set. Usually the crowd in his living room numbered in the double digits, and the program had some unknown carpenter make a box or something. Bud had a six-foot, hundred pound antenna on his roof to prove that he had a television set. It drew crowds to the lower duplex where he lived. Now we watch pretty much the same thing, and pay to have it delivered to the house.

The reason for living in the past like this is that I just parked my pontoon boat in a barn for the winter and realized that I am one of the last people on Maple Lake who still has tires hanging on his dock. No fancy store-bought bumpers, no boat lift. My tires are deteriorating. Another landmark will be passed. Soon there will be nothing left but steel belts hanging on the dock, and they won't do any good.

Why does everything have to change? What improved? Nothing, that's what. I still brush what's left of my teeth. There's still a carpenter on television but everyone stays home alone to watch him. The dang boat still has to be kept from smacking into the dock but now we have to buy bumpers and lifts.

Come to think of it, things are worse. If Grandma still had that doorknob full of rubber bands, I could hang it on the dock.

The Retiree—November, 2005—Luther

Well, I'm in trouble again. Wife said, "Do you still love me?" To prove how sincere I am, I quoted Martin Luther. Now I need to pick up some little memento to straighten out what is obviously a big misunderstanding. Something like the crown jewels of England should work.

She's been Lutheran long enough to know that Martin Luther wouldn't say anything offensive, unless maybe you happened to be the Pope or something. Maybe the quote wasn't applicable to the situation. That possibility exists.

What I said was, "Here I stand. I can do no other. God help me. Amen."

That didn't work too well for Luther, either, come to think of it. If I remember correctly, he had to go into hiding to keep his head attached. If I'd thought it through a little more thoroughly, I would have said something else, although quote memorization isn't my forté.

I could have said, "There are in these environs certain unscrupulous persons who, for a price, will perform the most unsavory tasks," which stuck in my head from an old movie, but that wouldn't have made any sense. Or "Quoth the raven, nevermore!" but that would have been worse. Another one that would have been good was "I tasted you, and I feel but hunger and thirst for you," by St. Augustine, but he wasn't talking about a wife. Emerson said "But in the mud and scum of things

There alway, alway something sings," but again, the thought conveyed would be a little confused.

I found a Vachel Lindsay poem that ended poem that ended "You are my love, if your heart is as kind as your young eyes now," and that would have been good enough before she got her new glasses, but I didn't have it memorized. Next time. When the opportunity presents itself I will no doubt default to Sandburg's "Gray gamblers, Handfuls again," and get myself into the same soup I'm in now with Luther.

Some people have a knack for coming up with the right words at the right time. I envy those people. When I am presented with a situation that requires quick thinking, my thought process is generally delayed for about a half hour. That probably caused my second retirement, as I would come up with a dandy response to a prospective client's objections just as I put the car in gear to drive away. Going back would have been dangerous as well as irresponsible so I retired instead. Was that chickening out? Or was I just acknowledging that I was better off retired than trying to fight a losing battle? But I digress. Now I'm trying to fight a different battle—but she wouldn't like that phrasing, either, as she doesn't look on marriage as a battle.

Luther's statement seems to have worked out for him in the long run. I hope the same thing applies to me. Some things should be left to settle down by themselves. She'll forget all about it in time, maybe.

I'm too old to be left alone here by the lake. Who'd help me pull the dock out if she left?

The Retiree—November, 2005—Letter

Every year I write a Christmas letter. Some people have requested a copy when they were somehow left off our mailing list. I'm not necessarily proud of that, as there are an equal number of people who ask to be skipped when I send out the next year's letter.

The reason some people like my letter is that I don't necessarily accentuate the positive. You won't find a list of great accomplishments there. I don't have any of those.

To save me from too much embarrassment, I'm going to show you only portions of past letters, and maybe give you a taste of this year's letter. Who knows; it could save me some postage. Here we go.

The story of our lives in 2005 was one of monotony, shallowness, misery, and depression, and we plan to recite every dull moment of it in this letter. Prepare yourself. But, in the spirit of Christmas, know that our Savior was born and that we stand acquitted of our offenses and free in our faith. Keep that in mind as you get increasingly ticked off by the pedestrian and totally inappropriate comments that follow.

We installed a screen door, finally, after which neighbors had a direct view from their porch to the vanity where we brush our teeth. As soon as they found that out, they arranged for the fire department to burn their house down. Evidently we aren't as attractive as we used to be.

We got a bee-killer thing that drowns bees in beer. Bees prefer

Leinenkugel's Creamy Dark Lager. Some were heard singing German drinking songs before they expired. The device didn't get them all, but it attracted a higher class of bee than we had before. We were careful around surviving bees. They were invariably hung over.

(This one is really REALLY old.) Steve has shown remarkable progress in the fifth grade. The teacher herself remarked on how far he'd gone, when the cops brought him back from Champlin. Hardly a day passes when he doesn't come home with some little kid's lunch money or a new book from the library.

I got a deer, using a 3.8 Buick instead of a .30-30 Winchester. Don't do it that way.

(Another really old one.) The 'h' keeps sticking on my manual typewriter so I'm going to use the 'k.'...We gave up on tke car and traded tke wortkless wreck off...wkick is a good buy...

Well, you get the idea. Like most people, we don't generally spend much time reading those multi-page letters that include honors and awards and proud parents. But people in general like to feel superior to someone, so lots of them read mine.

I don't mind. Most of the people who read my letter are superior to me, anyway.

The Retiree—December, 2005—Trip

Another trip came upon us. This one was no fun, as it was for an emergency in Missouri. But let's not dwell on that for now. The point of this column is Winter Travel, or WT.

Somehow I always get to drive someplace during the Storm of the Century, or SC for now, which seems to happen every year, sometimes twice. This time, the SC took place in Kansas City, or KC.

Our trip was on dry pavement to KC where we spent the night. Weather reports there indicated that 1—3 inches of snow was expected to come from CO to KS and then to MO, into KC the next day, so we knew we'd be OK if we left in the AM. Someone came into the motel and said he'd heard 7—10 inches of snow were expected but we thought that was, excuse the expression, BS.

We left early, watching snow build up on the highways. Snow was then beating up KC and causing a world-class traffic jam which is still being unraveled. You may not have seen that on the news. Nothing that happens in KC ever gets on the news. The drive was tense. Our consummate driving skills got us through.

With mission accomplished in Springfield, we drove to Eagle Rock, or ER, where relatives put us up. It was a good visit, but we had to leave early again, to make sure we got home in time for a granddaughter's concert. ER is on the edge of the Ozarks, where people drive big pickups with dualies on the back, and if they haven't run off the road in a month, figure that their macho-ness needs a tune-up.

The temperature was 17 when we left, and it was raining. Never, in several trips to those environs, have we seen dualie pickups driven so slowly. Nobody passed on curves or hills, or even on straight roads. Everybody had white knuckles, even those who were not white.

I got us through KC where the snowplows were driven by trainees. The storm had passed through MO and continued on to IA and IL. Since it appeared that we'd be getting into worse conditions, I did the only reasonable thing. I gave up the driving to my wife.

When we got to Des Moines, or DM, the results of SC and rookie driving were apparent. In one stretch of about a quarter mile, we counted 25 cars in the ditch. There were over 100 cars still ditched, and a similar number already enriching towtruck drivers. It was a scene of glorious disarray. Wife followed a semi being driven, apparently, by a native of Baja California or someplace else where snow has never been seen. After what seemed like a month, she was able to get around him and get us to a place where the roads were well maintained and people knew how to drive, namely MN.

If you leave MN for WT to KC or DM or ER, just remember that the SC can hit at any time and you'd be wise to do what our dog did on the trip. She went into suspended animation, let us do the worrying and driving, and refused food and water until she got home.

The Retiree—December, 2005—Skiing

Sliding into a graceful Telemark turn after a brief glissade across the blacktop by the garage, I launched into a dismount from the step rail toward a pyramidal juniper. Attempting an Immelmann turn but lacking airspeed, I went into a stall upon reaching the crest of the bush. From an upside down perspective I waved a cheery hello to Chive, who happened by in his greatcoat, bearskin hat and bunny boots. As I slid backwards down the shrub into the snow, it occurred to me that as a retiree I could be getting too old for anything involving skis or snow.

Chive opined, "Has it occurred to you that as a retiree you could be getting too old for anything involving skis or snow?"

"The thought just crossed my mind, as my life was passing before me," I commented, picking a rather well-structured branch out of my collar and trying to sit upright. "I may let others do the heavy lifting and resort to hot chocolate by the fire, watching out the window for skiers, a Bach fugue on the stereo."

"Bach fugue…is that the poisonous Japanese fish that people think is a delicacy until they croak? I'd prefer a dish of salted cashews and maybe a cup of coffee with possibly some rum slipped in when the wife is out of the room. And don't waste any time waiting for me to ski by your window. You may as well wait for this snow to melt. Come to think of it, I'm waiting for this snow to melt, too."

"No, the fish is fugu, not fugue, and it doesn't go well with chocolate,

I suspect, although I never plan to test it out," I said, using part of a shattered ski pole to get juniper berries out of my ears. "What sort of exercise do you do?"

"I haven't been retired as many times as you, but even in my inexperience I find that serving as a pall bearer gives me all the arm exercise I need. As for walking, I usually end up on the wrong side of the gas hose and have to walk around the whole car to put it away, no small task since I became Buick-eligible. Strength tests include putting out the garbage almost every week, and opening a lot of bottles and cans. Need any help there with the dog poop on your back?"

"Ya, thanks, use that ice chisel over there, and then take a swipe at the part of my right ski that's still attached to the steps. It'll make good kindling. I'm thinking I should reduce my winter activity to things related to removing snow instead of playing in it. The snowblower is more fun anyway. Once in awhile I can blow acorns all the way to the road. I snorted a juniper berry from my left nostril nearly that far just now."

It helps to have neighbors who can renew a perspective on life. My own devices often mislead me into untoward activities. Old hockey skates are hanging on a nail under the basement steps. With a little luck, I can drive the nail in so close that they'll never come off again. Does anyone need a left ski and one pole?